The Road to Nirvana

The Road to Nirvana

*A selection of the Buddhist Scriptures
translated from the Pali by*

E. J. Thomas, *M.A., D.Litt.*

Charles E. Tuttle Company
Boston • Rutland, Vermont • Tokyo

Published in the United States in 1992 by
Charles E. Tuttle Company, Inc. of
Rutland, Vermont & Tokyo, Japan with editorial offices
at 77 Central Street, Boston, Massachusetts 02109.

Library of Congress Catalog Card Number 91-78173

ISBN 0-8048-1796-0

*This is a facsimile edition of the work originally published
in London by John Murray in 1950.*

PRINTED IN THE UNITED STATES

CONTENTS

EDITORIAL NOTE

WHEN the Wisdom of the East Series first appeared in the early part of this century, it introduced the rich heritage of Eastern thought to Western readers. Spanning time and place from ancient Egypt to Imperial Japan, it carries the words of Buddha, Confucius, Lao Tzu, Muhammad, and other great spiritual leaders. Today, in our time of increased tension between East and West, it is again important to publish these classics of Eastern philosophy, religion, and poetry. In doing so, we hope The Wisdom of the East Series will serve as a bridge of understanding between cultures, and continue to emulate the words of its founding editor, J. L. Cranmer-Byng:

> *[I] desire above all things that these books shall be the ambassadors of good-will between East and West, [and] hope that they will contribute to a fuller knowledge of the great cultural heritage of the East.*

INTRODUCTION

ONE of the most remarkable facts in the history of Buddhism is that the course of its career in India has been almost unknown to the West until modern times. Buddhism first came into the light of history in the third century B.C. with the missionary zeal of the emperor Asoka. For over a thousand years it continued to flourish in India. It developed schools, and forged its logical weapons to repel the attacks of Hindu philosophers, and it extended its teaching over large areas of central Asia, China, and Japan. Yet when the West began to inquire into the actual origin and spread of the religion there was little to be found beyond legends and travellers' tales.

At the end of the eighteenth century a few scholars made attempts to describe it from Chinese sources. Some documents were recovered from the Tibetan and also a few works in Sanskrit, but all from very late schools. There was nothing which allowed investigators to arrive at the historical facts of the origin of the religion and its growth for two thousand years.

Then in the middle of the nineteenth century came the discovery of the Pāli Buddhism of Ceylon. Everything was put in a fresh light. Here was a complete canon of the Scriptures certainly earlier than anything known before. There were also histories in Pāli, the sacred language, describing the events of the first community down to the time of Asoka. Best of all, as the date of Chandragupta, the grandfather of Asoka, was known, the events of Indian history no longer floated in a sea of undatable mythology, but could be compared with the chronology of the West. We now know that the Pāli Canon does not stand alone. For centuries the chief growth of Buddhism was in India, and we find that all known schools of Buddhism had essentially the same Canon. It was preserved by memory, so that differences of arrangement appear, but it contains no trace of the dogmatic differences of the schools. By one school it was translated into Sanskrit, and this now exists in Chinese and Tibetan versions. But more and more of the original Sanskrit is being discovered. The result is to show a common body of doctrinal teaching with a legendary setting, which developed in varying ways in the commentaries.

It is the legendary setting which has always made Buddhism attractive. The young prince brought up to be a great monarch, carefully shielded from any knowledge of the dark side of human existence, his sudden realizing of the facts of old age, sickness, and death, his renunciation of worldly joys, and his discovery of a way of escape—all this is legend, but it is legend which enshrines the spiritual experience of one of the great personalities of the world, the Buddha, the enlightened one, whose teaching penetrated India and swept over vast regions of Asia.

No one doubts that Buddha founded an Order of monks, and for many years preached to all classes of people. It is also certain that these disciples collected all that they remembered of his discourses. All schools have held and still hold that the Master taught four truths : the fact of pain or ill, its origin, its cessation, and the way by which it can be made to cease. And this cessation results in a state of bliss, Nirvāṇa. It is a remarkable fact that, in spite of all the disputes due to the rise of new problems and the changes that might be expected as the teaching spread among various peoples, these doctrines have remained—the four Truths, the Way, and Nirvāṇa.

The discovery of the Pāli Scriptures has not solved all problems, but it has given us a definite stage at which a system of doctrines was taught as being the word of Buddha. Whatever investigations may be necessary, it seems to be all the more important first to make sure what the Buddhists actually say, and what they believe to be the Master's teaching. These Scriptures are the starting-point. In the Pāli Canon we have the only complete collection now existing in an Indian language. It is known as the *Tipiṭaka*, " The Threefold Basket ".

THE SCRIPTURES

1. *Vinaya-piṭaka*. The Basket of Discipline. The basis of this is the list of 227 rules for the Order of monks and nuns, graded according to their importance, the first four, violation of which involves expulsion from the Order, being (1) incontinence, (2) theft, (3) taking life or persuading to suicide, (4) false boasting of supernatural attainments. The rules also exist in a separate form (the *Pātimokkha*), and are recited at the fortnightly meetings of the Order.

Then follow the *Khandhakas*, two sections of rules for admission to the Order, daily regulations, the mode of treating offences, and a supplement, the *Parivāra*, giving summaries. The whole is accompanied by a commentary explaining how each rule came to be established, and much legendary matter is included. As the commentarial matter continued to grow, it took various forms in different schools with the incorporation of additional legends, the whole of which is now reckoned as Scripture.

2. *Sutta-piṭaka*. The Basket of discourses or *Dhamma*, the doctrine. This is in five divisions (*nikāyas*).

(i) *Dīgha-nikāya*. Division of long discourses.

(ii) *Majjhima-nikāya*. Division of medium-long discourses.

(iii) *Saṃyutta-nikāya*. Division of connected discourses.

(iv) *Anguttara-nikāya*. In this division there are eleven

groups, in the first of which there is one subject in each discourse, in the second two, and so on up to eleven. Hence the name, ' one member in addition '.

(v) *Khuddaka-nikāya*. Division of minor discourses. This is peculiar to the Pāli, but some of the items included in it exist as separate works in other schools. It contains the anthology of verses widely known as the *Dhammapada*, " Words of the Doctrine ", and several collections of moral tales, the best known being the *Jātaka*, stories of Buddha's previous births.

3. *Abhidhamma-piṭaka*. The basket of further Dhamma, discussions of principles and special doctrines in seven works. The principles are in a sense the word of Buddha, but the discussions are elaborate treatises which must have been compiled in the monastic places of instruction. Other schools had an Abhidhamma of similar matter, but quite distinct from the Pāli.

What we find in the Scriptures is not merely a number of new doctrines, but the picture of a people with their views about the facts of daily life, their beliefs about their social and religious duties, their theories of the gods, and the question of a future existence. This is the common Indian background. Buddhism was not a system which replaced all this. The monk as well as the layman shared the general views of the nature of the world and man, so far as they were not in conflict with the doctrine. Two of these views already generally held were the doctrine of karma and the belief in rebirth or reincarnation. Karma (action) is the belief that every deliberately willed action will receive its reward or punishment. It is a view that belongs to many religions, but it receives a much deeper significance when combined with the doctrine of rebirth. Recompense for actions is not always evident, but the idea becomes conceivable when combined with the belief in a former existence and the prospect of another life, in which the fruit of past actions may be reaped. Buddhism accepted this view and emphasized it.

> Of no one is the deed destroyed,
> It comes, indeed its master meets it;
> In the next world the sinful fool
> Suffers in his own self the pain.

Good deeds might lead to heaven, but even such bliss lasted only until the accumulated merit was exhausted, and the wheel of birth turned again. The problem for Buddha was the same that faced everyone. Is there a way of escape from rebirth? Already teachers had arisen who claimed to have found a way. There was the doctrine of the Upanishads, which made union with the one reality the goal. This is never mentioned by the Buddhists, and was probably unknown to them, as it was a secret doctrine taught to initiates. We hear of a number of other teachers, who had their own theories of man's destiny and of the means of release. The best known of these are the Jains, who aimed at the annihilation of karma. Buddha claimed to have discovered an original way, " a doctrine unheard before ".

This doctrine, being a way or method, is not, in the first place, a creed, but a course of mental training. The great aim is to get rid of all the evil tendencies of the individual, which hinder him from seeing things as they are. In this the system was unlike such religions as aimed at appeasing a deity by sacrifices or at finding salvation by annihilating karma. Instead it set forth a scheme of self-training within the reach of everyone. To see things as they really are means seeing them as taught by the truths of Buddhism, and to that extent Buddhism involves a creed. It begins with a belief in the impermanence and continual change of everything in the universe including the gods. But this is combined with the belief in a permanent state of peace to be attained, the goal of Nirvāṇa. Mere belief is not enough. The truths must be known, meditated upon, and understood, until they are realized with absolute conviction. This requires a course of training.

We find schemes of training expressed in various ways, and doubtless there has been much scholastic elaboration. They all rest upon one plan. First a training in morality, followed by the practice of meditation intended to develop the latent powers of the individual and to discard the fetters, the inborn vices and wrong views which hinder insight. The last stage is full knowledge : " he reflects on himself as purified from all these bad and evil qualities, he reflects on himself as released. As he reflects on himself thus purified and released, exultation arises, as he exults joy arises, with his mind full of joy his body is calmed ; when his body is calmed he feels happiness, and being happy his mind is concentrated." [1] He has become an arahat.

The same triple division is implied in the Noble Eightfold Way,[2] for right speech, right action, and right livelihood constitute morality ; the mental training is included in right effort, right mindfulness, and right concentration ; and the culmination of full knowledge is found in right resolve and right view. But morality is never merely preparatory. There is a discourse which declares that unless ten things are put away, passion, hate, delusion, anger, ill-will, hypocrisy, spite, jealousy, greed, and pride, it is impossible to realize arahatship.

The stages of progress along the Way, as the disciple casts off the fetters, are four :

Entering the Stream. He who has entered the stream casts off belief in a permanent individuality, doubt, and belief in mere morality and rites.

The Once-returner, as he reduces or casts off further fetters, will be reborn once more in this world.

---

[1] *Majjhima*, i. 2 and 3.   [2] See the First Sermon, p. 27.

The Non-returner will not return to this world, but will be re-born in the formless world, and from there make an end of pain.

The Arahat, the perfected one (lit. worthy), who has destroyed the three fundamental corruptions known as the *āsavas*, passion, desire for becoming, and ignorance, is released with the attainment of full knowledge.

The perfected disciple has reached a permanent state of peace, something absolute as opposed to the process of constant change. This state is Nirvāṇa, lit. ' blowing out, extinction '. Extinction of what? Extinction of craving (*taṇhā*, thirst) with its three roots, passion, desire for becoming, and ignorance. Nirvāṇa has been interpreted by some Westerners as implying the extinction of the individual at death. For this there is no evidence either in the Scriptures or in any of the interpretations given by the commentators. On the contrary it is expressly denied that there is annihilation (*uccheda*, lit. cutting off) or destruction of a released person at the dissolution of the body, so that he should not exist after death. The released disciple may declare his bliss, but what the state is never receives positive expression. It is a state of permanence as opposed to the process of continual change or becoming (*saṃsāra*), which is all that we experience, and only he who has attained it can know it.

In its contact with other systems Buddhism was compelled to face certain metaphysical and ontological questions. Some of these, known as the Undetermined Questions, were put aside as useless for the disciple intent on release. (*See* Ch. XIV.) The question of the self receives special treatment. When it is a matter of the self of actual experience this is never denied. This self is analysed into five groups. But the Jains and Hindus held that behind these was a permanent, unchanging entity, an *ātman*, which transmigrates. It is this sense of the word *ātman*, self or soul, which is denied. (*See* Ch. XV.)

It was the continual insistence on morality that gave the new teaching its appeal to lay people. Buddha is represented as beginning his discourses to the multitude by preaching on morality, on the folly of the passions, and on the hope of heaven. He did not speak of the doctrine until their minds were prepared for it. But even his moral discourses were not merely the old teaching. They were a new gospel preached by one inspired with new moral ideals. The old belief in *dharma*, the theory of man's duty in all relations of life, involved much of merely ritual value. Buddha by emphasizing the true moral character of action, the motive, was able to show the insignificance or the error of mere ritual, or even to preach against it, as in denouncing animal sacrifices. There are many instances of Buddha's wisdom in dealing with individual characters and developing their higher impulses, as in the story of the farmer who, after searching for a strayed ox, came late and wearied to hear Buddha preach. The Master waited for him, and ordered that he should first receive some food. Such stories, even when not properly historical, show how the new ideals had penetrated the moral consciousness of his hearers.

It is well known that Buddhism in India itself split up into schools, and one branch underwent the great development known as Mahāyāna, " the great career ", as it now exists in China and Japan. It extended the doctrine of impermanence into the view that everything but Nirvāṇa is " void " or empty of reality, so that nothing as perceived in the changing world can be called real at all. But its chief feature, from which it takes its name, is that the disciple ought to aim not directly at release, but at the Great Career (*mahā-yāna*) of a bodhisatta, and finally become a Buddha. But, even so, and it is a fact not always recognized, the end remains the same, for the final aim of all bodhisattas and Buddhas is the attainment of Nirvāṇa.

I. THE DREAM OF QUEEN MĀYĀ

GOTAMA, the future Buddha, was born as the son of the Rājā of the tribe of the Sakyas at Kapilavatthu on the borders of Nepal. The Ceylon reckoning makes the date 624 B.C. This would make the date of his death at the age of eighty 544 B.C., and the Buddhists of Ceylon make 543 B.C. the first year of their era. Western scholars reckoning backwards from the known date of Asoka usually place it sixty years later, 483 B.C.

The following account, however, belongs not to history, but to the legend in which had developed the doctrine of a bodhisatta. A bodhisatta (a being destined for enlightenment) is one who has made a vow to become in some future existence a Buddha. Before his last birth, while still in the Tusita heaven, he chooses to be born and attain enlightenment, so that his birth is quite independent of any earthly father. This became the common doctrine of all the schools.

THEN was proclaimed in the city of Kapilavatthu the midsummer festival of the month Āsālha, and many persons celebrated the festival. The queen Mahāmāyā, beginning from the seven days before the full moon, celebrated the festival with the splendour of garlands and perfumes, and without the drinking of intoxicants. On the seventh day she rose early, bathed in scented water, bestowed a great gift of 400,000 pieces of money as alms, being adorned with all kinds of ornaments, ate of choice food, took upon her the fast-day vows, and entered the splendidly adorned royal bedchamber. Lying on the royal bed she fell asleep, and dreamt this dream : The four Great Kings [1] raised her together with the bed, and took her to the Himalaya to the Manosilā tableland, sixty leagues in length, and placing her beneath a great sāl-tree seven leagues high, they stood on one side.

[1] The four World-guardians, gods of the four quarters.

9   B

Then their queens approached and took the queen to the lake
Anotattā, bathed her to remove human stain, robed her in a
divine dress, anointed her with perfumes, and decked her with
divine flowers. Not far from there is Silver mountain and on
it a golden palace. There they prepared and set a divine bed
with its head to the east. Then the Bodhisatta became a white
elephant. Not far from there is a certain Golden mountain,
and the Bodhisatta went there, descended from it, ascended
Silver mountain, approaching it from the north, and in his trunk
like a silver chain he bore a white lotus. He trumpeted, entered
the golden palace, made a rightwise circuit three times round
his mother's bed, smote her right side, and seemed to enter her
womb. Thus at the end of the midsummer festival he received
a new existence.

The next day on awaking the queen told her dream to the
king. The king summoned sixty-four famous brahmins, caused
the ground to be strewn with festive lāja-flowers, prepared
splendid seats, filled the gold and silver bowls of the brahmins
seated there with cooked ghee, honey, sugar, and excellent rice,
and gave it to them covered with gold and silver covers. He
also delighted them with other gifts, such as new clothes and
tawny cows. Then when they were delighted with all these
pleasures, he related the dream. "What will take place?" he
asked. The brahmins said, "King, be not anxious, the queen
has conceived, and the child will be a male, not a female. You
will have a son, and if he lives a household life he will become
a universal monarch ; and if he leaves his house and goes forth
from the world he will become a Buddha, a dispeller of illusion
in the world."

(*Jātaka, Introd.*, i. 50 ff.)

II. THE BIRTH OF GOTAMA

GOTAMA is the name of the whole clan (*gotra*) to which Buddha belonged, so that it is a kind of surname. He was of the warrior caste and Gotama (Skt. Gautama) is a Brahmin name, possibly the gotra of the brahmin who performed the religious rites. His personal name was Siddhattha or Siddhārtha, " he who has accomplished his aim ". By the Buddhists he is called Bodhisatta up to the time of his enlightenment, and is afterwards addressed as Bhagavā, " Lord ". He is represented as referring to himself as the Tathāgata, lit. " one who has gone thus ", and interpreted to mean one who has gone like previous Buddhas. But this sense is never emphasized in the Scriptures, which use it especially in referring to the Lord's special powers, and hence Lord Chalmers's translation " he who has won truth " more fairly represents its actual use.

THE queen Mahāmāyā, bearing the Bodhisatta like oil in a vessel for ten (lunar) months, desired, when her time was come, to go to her relatives' home, and addressed king Suddhodana : " Your Majesty, I wish to go to Devadaha, the city of my people." " Good," replied the king, and he caused the road from Kapilavatthu to the city of Devadaha to be made smooth, adorned it with plantains in pots, flags and banners, seated the queen in a golden palanquin borne by a thousand courtiers, and sent her forth with a great retinue. Between the two cities, and belonging to the inhabitants of both, is a pleasure-grove of sāl-trees, called the Lumbini-grove. At that time, from the roots to the tips of the branches, the whole grove was in full flower, and among the branches and flowers were numberless bees of the five colours, and flocks of various kinds of birds, singing with sweet sounds. The whole Lumbini-grove seemed like the heavenly Cittalatā-grove or like an adorned banqueting pavilion for a mighty king.

When the queen saw it, the desire arose in her heart of sporting therein. The courtiers took the queen and entered the sāl-grove. She went to the foot of a royal sāl-tree, and desired to take hold of a branch. The sāl-tree branch, like the tip of a supple reed, bowed down and came within reach of the queen's hand. She put out her hand and seized the branch. Then she was shaken by the pangs of birth. The multitude put round her a curtain and retired. Taking hold of the sāl-branch and standing up she was delivered. And even at that moment the four pure-minded Mahābrahmās [members of the heaven of Brahmā] came and brought a golden net, and with the golden net they received the Bodhisatta and set him before his mother, saying, " Rejoice, O queen, a mighty son is born to thee." And as other beings at their birth are born with disagreeable impurity and stain, so was not the Bodhisatta. But the Bodhisatta, like a preacher of the doctrine descending from his seat of doctrine, like a man descending stairs, stretched forth his two hands and feet, and standing unsoiled, unstained, and free from any impurity from the sojourn of his birth, like a jewel placed in Benares cloth, thus brilliant did he descend from his mother. And yet in honour of the Bodhisatta and the Bodhisatta's mother two showers of water descended from the sky and performed the regular ceremony on the bodies of the Bodhisatta and his mother. Then from the hands of the Brahmās, who stood and received him in a golden net, the four Great Kings received him on a ceremonial robe of antelope skin soft to the touch, and from their hands human beings received him on a silken cushion, and when he was freed from the hands of human beings he stood on the earth and looked at the eastern quarter. Gods and men then worshipped him with scented garlands, and said, " Great Being, there is here none like thee, much less superior anywhere." So having examined the four quarters, the intermediate quarters, the nadir and the zenith, ten quarters, and not seeing anyone like himself, he said, " this is the supreme quarter", and took seven steps. While Mahābrahmā held a white parasol over him, and Suyāma a fan, and other divinities followed with the other symbols of royalty in their hands, he stopped at the seventh step, and raising his lordly voice, " I am the chief in the world," he roared his lion-roar.

(*Jātaka, Introd.*, i. 52.)

III. THE FOUR SIGNS

OWING to the prophecy of the brahmins made to Suddhodana that his son would become either a universal king or a Buddha, the king is said to have built three palaces for him and to have tried to conceal from him the ills of human life. The same story is told in the Scriptures in the Mahāpadāna discourse of one of the previous Buddhas Vipassin, for the same essential stages in the progress to enlightenment are experience by all Buddhas.

Now one day, when the Bodhisatta desired to go into the park, he called his charioteer, and said, " Yoke the chariot." " Very good," he replied, and adorning a great and most excellent chariot with all adornments, yoked the four royal Sindh horses of the colour of white lotus-petals and informed the Bodhisatta. The Bodhisatta mounted the chariot, which was like a vehicle of the gods, and went towards the park. The gods thought, " The time for the enlightenment of prince Siddhattha is near, we will show him a previous sign," and they caused a son of the gods to appear, infirm with age, broken-toothed, grey-haired, bent, with crooked body, leaning on a staff, trembling, and showed him. But only the Bodhisatta and the charioteer saw him. Then the Bodhisatta asked the charioteer in the way recorded in the Mahāpadāna discourse, " Friend, who is that man, even his hair is not like that of others ? " And on hearing his reply said, " Woe upon birth, since through it old age must come upon one that is born," and with troubled heart he returned from thence and entered the palace. The king asked, " Why does my son return so quickly ? " They said, " Your Majesty, he has seen an old man, and he is going to retire from the world." " Why will you kill me ? Prepare stage-plays for my son quickly ; if he obtains happiness, he will have no thought of leaving the world," said the king. And he prepared a guard, and set them in all directions to the distance of half a league.

Again on a certain day, as the Bodhisatta in the same way was going to the park, he saw a diseased man set there by the gods, and having asked as before he returned with troubled heart and entered the palace. The king also inquired as before said, and again prepared a guard and put them on all sides to the distance of three-quarters of a league. Again on another day the Bodhisatta when going in the same way to the park saw a corpse put there by the gods, and having asked as before he returned again with troubled heart to the palace. The king also inquired as before said, and again prepared a guard and put them on all sides to the distance of a league. Again another day when going to the park in the same way saw put there by the gods a man who had left the world, carefully and duly dressed. " Friend, who is this ? " he asked the charioteer. As it was not the time of the appearance of a Buddha, the charioteer knew nothing of one who had left the world or of the virtues of leaving the world, but through the power of the gods he replied, " Your Highness, that is a man who has left the world," and he described the virtues of leaving the world. The Bodhisatta was delighted with the thought of leaving the world, and that day he went on through the park. But the reciters of the Dīgha (Collection of long discourses) say that he went and saw the four signs all on one day.

(*Jātaka, Introd.*, i. 58 ff.)

IV. THE GREAT RENUNCIATION

GOTAMA at the age of sixteen was married to his cousin Yasodharā. At the age of twenty-nine, on the day when he had seen the man who had left the world and was returning to the city, the news of his son's birth was announced to him. In the Pāli accounts his wife is described in very attractive terms. When Buddha after his enlightenment paid a visit to his home, all the women except Yasodharā went to see him. She said, "If I have any excellence, my Master will come to my presence, and when he comes I will reverence him." Buddha went with the two chief disciples to her chamber, and "she came swiftly, clasped his ankles, placed his feet round her head, and did reverence to him according to her desire". Both she and Rāhula are said to have entered the Order.

AT that time, on hearing that the mother of Rāhula[1] had borne a son, king Suddhodana sent the message, "Announce the happy news to my son." The Bodhisatta, when he heard, said, "Rāhula is born, a fetter is born." The king asked, "What did my son say?" and on hearing said, "Henceforth let the name of my grandson be prince Rāhula." But the Bodhisatta mounted a splendid chariot and entered the city with great honour and most delightful glory. At that time a girl of the warrior caste named Kisā Gotamī had gone to the top of the palace, and beheld the beauty and glory of the Bodhisatta, as he made a rightwise procession round the city; and filled with joy and delight she made this solemn utterance :

[1] The name is a diminutive of Rāhu, the demon who swallows the sun or moon at an eclipse. The meaning "impediment" seems to be implied here.

Happy [1] indeed is the mother,
Happy indeed is the father,
Happy indeed is the wife,
Who has such a husband as he.

The Buddha heard, and thought, " Even so she spoke. On seeing such a form a mother's heart becomes happy, a father's heart becomes happy, a wife's heart becomes happy. Now when what is extinguished (*nibbuta*) is the heart happy (*nibbuta*) ? " And with aversion in his mind for the passions he thought, " When the fire of lust is extinguished it is happy, when the fire of hate, of illusion is extinguished it is happy, when pride, false views, and all passions and pains are extinguished it is happy. She has taught me a good lesson, for I am searching for extinguishment (*nibbāna*). Even to-day I must reject and renounce a household life and go forth from the world to seek extinguishment. Let this be her fee for teaching." And loosing from his neck a pearl necklace worth 100,000 pieces, he sent it to Kisā Gotamī. She thought that prince Siddhattha was in love with her and had sent her a present, and she was filled with delight. But the Bodhisatta with great glory and majesty went up to his palace and lay down on the royal bed.

At that time beautiful women decked with all kinds of adornments, well trained in dancing, singing, and so on, had taken various musical instruments, and came round him, diverting him with their dancing, singing, and music. The Bodhisatta through his mind being averse to the passions took no pleasure in the dancing and music, and fell asleep for a short time. The women thought. " He for whose sake we are dancing and

---

[1] *Nibbuta :* it is connected with two verbs, so that it can mean either " happy " or " extinguished ", and the noun *nibbāna* (Skt. *nirvāṇa*) can mean " happiness " or " extinction ". The Bodhisatta here plays upon the two meanings.

singing has fallen asleep ; why do we now weary ourselves ? "
And taking their instruments they strewed them about and lay
down. Lamps of perfumed oil were burning. The Bodhisatta
on waking up sat cross-legged on the bed, and saw the women
sleeping with their instruments thrown about, some with phlegm
trickling and their bodies wet with spittle, some grinding their
teeth, some snoring, some muttering, some with open mouths,
some with their dress fallen apart, and repulsive parts disclosed.
On seeing their disgraceful appearance he was still more averse
to pleasures. The hall, though adorned and decorated like the
palace of Sakka, seemed to him like a cemetery filled with all
sorts of corpses strewn about, and the three modes of existence
appeared like a house on fire. His solemn utterance broke forth,
" How oppressive, how afflicting," and his thought turned
mightily to abandoning the world.

Thinking, " To-day I must make the great renunciation,"
he rose from his bed and went towards the door. " Who is
there ? " he said. Channa, who had put his head on the threshold, said, " Noble sir, it is I, Channa." " To-day I wish to
make the great renunciation ; saddle me a horse." Channa
replied, " Good, your highness," and taking the horse-trappings
he went to the stable, and by the light of scented oil-lamps he
saw Kanthaka, the king of horses, standing in a goodly stall
beneath a jasmine-flowered canopy. " This is the one I must
saddle to-day," he said, and he saddled Kanthaka. The horse,
as he was being saddled, thought, " This is very tight harness ;
it is not like harness used on other days in going for pleasure
in the park. My noble master must to-day be wishing to make
the great renunciation." So with delighted mind he gave a
great neigh. The sound would have extended through the
whole city, but the gods suppressed the sound and allowed no
one to hear.

When the Bodhisatta had sent Channa, he thought, " Now I will go and see my son," and rising from where he was sitting cross-legged he went to the room of Rāhula's mother, and opened the door. At that moment a scented oil-lamp was burning in the room. The mother of Rāhula was sleeping on a bed strewn with a mass of jasmine and other flowers, and with her hand on her son's head. The Bodhisatta put his foot on the threshold and stood looking. "If I move the queen's hand and take my son, the queen will awake. Thus there will be an obstacle to my going. When I have become a Buddha I will come and see him." And he went down from the palace.

(With Channa riding behind him he passed through the city-gates, which were opened by divine beings, and rode as far as the river Anomā. There he crossed the river, cut off his hair, and sent Channa back with the horse.)

But the horse Kanthaka, who stood listening to the voice of the Bodhisatta, as he deliberated with Channa, thought, " Now I shall never see my master again." And when he passed out of sight he was unable to bear the grief, and his heart broke, and he died and was born again in the heaven of the Thirty-three gods as a son of the gods named Kanthaka.

At first Channa had had one grief, but when Kanthaka died he was overcome by a second grief, and returned weeping and lamenting to the city.

(*Jātaka, Introd.*, i. 60 ff.)

V. THE ENLIGHTENMENT

GOTAMA on his renunciation went to Rājagaha, the capital of the Magadhas, where he is said to have studied under several teachers without result. Then for six years he practised severe penance with five disciples, but finding self-mortification useless he abandoned it, whereupon his disciples left him. He went and sat down under a pipal-tree, the Bodhi-tree, tree of enlightenment, vowing not to rise until he had won enlightenment. Here the commentaries and later works give the story of the temptation by Māra, the god of the world of sense enjoyments, who came to turn him from his purpose. We are told that he meditated, attained the four stages of trance, acquired the memory of his past births, the knowledge of the destinies of beings, and the destruction of the *āsavas*, the corruptions, which are explained to be sensual desire, desire for becoming, and ignorance.

In the earliest accounts of the Enlightenment there is no mention of the Chain of Causation, but as it became the standard expression of the doctrine of causal change it is naturally placed by the commentators as being thought out under the Bodhi-tree. It is a detailed statement of the truths of the origin of pain and of its cessation. The formula has been the subject of much research, but it will here be sufficient to give the usual Buddhist interpretation. The links of the series are explained as stages of the individual, as he passes from birth to birth, and it includes three existences. The first is a past birth : an individual through ignorance becomes reborn, and passes with the aggregates of his existence to form a new individual. Then in the form of consciousness (rebirth-consciousness) he is reborn again and becomes an individual with mind and body (name and form). He acquires the six senses, which develop contact (the special activity of each), then feeling, craving, and grasping or clinging to existence ; and with the desire of becoming he passes to a new birth, to old age and death, and the series begins anew.

In the oldest comment in the Canon (*Dīgha*, ii. 63) the series starts with birth-consciousness, and the chief difficulty about actual rebirth is there made clear : " If consciousness did not descend into the mother's womb, would mind and body be consolidated in the mother's womb ?" " No, Lord." But consciousness is not conceived as a permanent element passing unchanged from birth to birth. It is only part of the complex of the individual, and in constant change with the other elements it takes that special form at the time of rebirth.

THE FOUR TRANCES

HAVING taken solid food and gained strength, without sensual desires and evil ideas, I attained and abode in the first trance, which is accompanied with reasoning and investigation, arising from seclusion, and full of joy and pleasure. With the ceasing of reasoning and investigation I attained and abode in the second trance of internal serenity, with mind fixed on one point, without reasoning and investigation, arising from concentration, and full of joy and pleasure. With equanimity towards joy and aversion I abode mindful and conscious, and experienced bodily pleasure, what the noble ones describe as, abiding with equanimity, mindful and happy, and I attained and abode in the third trance. Abandoning pleasure and abandoning pain, even before the disappearance of elation and depression, I attained and abode in the fourth trance, which is without pain and pleasure, and with purity of equanimity and mindfulness.

MEMORY OF FORMER EXISTENCES

Thus with mind concentrated, purified, cleansed, spotless, with the defilements gone, supple, dexterous, firm, and impassible, I directed my mind to the knowledge of the remembrance of my former existences. I remembered many former existences, such as one birth, two, three, four, five, ten, twenty, thirty, forty, fifty, a hundred, a thousand, a hundred thousand births ;

many cycles of dissolution of the universe, many cycles of its evolution ; many of its dissolution and evolution ; there was I of such and such a name, clan, colour, livelihood, suffering such pleasure and pain, and having such end of life. Passing away thence I was born elsewhere. There too I was of such and such a name, clan, colour, livelihood, suffering such pleasure and pain, and having such end of life. Passing away thence I was reborn here. Thus do I remember my former existences with their special modes and details. This was the first knowledge that I gained in the first watch of the night.

THE DIVINE EYE

Thus with mind concentrated, purified, cleansed, spotless, with the defilements gone, supple, dexterous, firm, and impassible, I directed my mind to the passing away and rebirth of beings. With divine, purified, superhuman vision I saw beings passing away and being reborn, low and high, of good and bad colour, in happy or miserable existences, according to their karma. Those beings who have led evil lives in deed, word, or thought, speaking evil of the noble ones, holders of false views, who acquire karma through their false views, at the dissolution of the body after death are reborn in a state of misery and suffering in hell. But those beings who have led good lives in deed, word, and thought, speaking no evil of the noble ones, of right views, who acquire karma through their right views, at the dissolution of the body after death are reborn in a happy state in the world of heaven. This was the second knowledge that I gained in the middle watch of the night.

DESTRUCTION OF THE ĀSAVAS

Thus with mind concentrated, purified, cleansed, spotless, with the defilements gone, supple, dexterous, firm, and impassible,

I directed my mind to the knowledge of the destruction of the corruptions (*āsavas*). I duly realized : this is pain. I duly realized : this is the cause of pain. I duly realized : this is the cessation of pain. I duly realized : this is the way that leads to the cessation of pain. I duly realized : these are the corruptions. I duly realized : this is the cause of the corruptions. I duly realized : this is the cessation of the corruptions. I duly realized : this is the way that leads to the cessation of the corruptions. As I thus knew and thus perceived, my mind was released from the corruption of sensual desire, from the corruption of desire for becoming, from the corruption of ignorance. In (me) released arose the knowledge that I was released. I realized that destroyed is rebirth, the religious life has been led, done what was to be done, there is nothing further for this existence. This was the third knowledge that I gained in the third watch of the night.

(*Majjhima*, i. 247.)

THE CHAIN OF CAUSATION

At that time the Lord Buddha was dwelling at Uruvelā on the banks of the Neranjarā, at the foot of the Bodhi-tree, just after he had attained complete enlightenment. Now the Lord sat cross-legged at the foot of the Bodhi-tree for seven days, experiencing the bliss of emancipation. So the Lord during the first watch of the night meditated on the chain of causation in direct and in reverse order : from ignorance come the aggregates [elements of the individual], from the aggregates consciousness, from consciousness name and form [mind and body], from mind and body the six organs of sense [the five senses and mind or the inner sense], from the organs of sense contact, from contact feeling, from feeling craving, from craving clinging to existence, from clinging to existence the desire of becoming, from the desire of becoming rebirth, from rebirth old age and death, grief, lamentation, pain, sorrow, and despair. Such is the origin of the whole mass of suffering.

Now from the complete and trackless cessation of ignorance there is the cessation of the aggregates, from the cessation of the aggregates there is the cessation of consciousness, from the cessation of consciousness there is the cessation of mind and body, from the cessation of mind and body there is the cessation of the six senses, from the cessation of the six senses there is the cessation of contact, from the cessation of contact there is the cessation of feeling, from the cessation of feeling there is the cessation of craving, from the cessation of craving the cessation of clinging to existence, from the cessation of clinging to existence there is the cessation of the desire of becoming, from the cessation of the desire of becoming there is the cessation of rebirth, from the cessation of rebirth old age, death, grief, lamentation, pain, sorrow, and despair cease. Even so is the cessation of this entire mass of pain.

(*Vinaya, Mahāv.*, i. 1.)

VI. THE FIRST PREACHING

BUDDHA after spending seven weeks at the Bodhi-tree, and having decided to begin his preaching, went to Benares, where he knew that his five former disciples were staying. Here he is said to have preached his first sermon, " the Discourse of setting in motion the Wheel of the Doctrine ", in which are taught the four Truths and the Noble Eightfold Way.

Now the Lord by gradual journeying came to Benares, to the Isipatana deer-park, where were the five monks. The five monks saw the Lord coming from afar, and on seeing him decided among themselves, " This, friends, is the ascetic Gotama coming, who lives in abundance, who has given up exertion, and turned to a life of abundance. We must not address him, nor rise to greet him, nor take his bowl and robe, but a seat may be set for him. If he wishes he may sit down." But as the Lord approached the five monks, so the five monks did not abide by their agreement, but went to meet the Lord, and one took the Lord's bowl and robe, one arranged a seat, one set water for his feet, a footstool, and a cloth. The Lord sat on the appointed seat, and on sitting down the Lord washed his feet. Then they addressed the Lord by name, and by the title of 'friend'. Thereat the Lord said to the five monks, " Do not, monks, address the Tathāgata by name, nor by the title of 'friend'. The Tathāgata, monks, is an arahat, and has obtained complete enlightenment. Give ear, monks, I have attained the immortal ; I instruct, I teach the doctrine. If you so walk according to what is taught, you will yourselves in no long time realize in this life with higher knowledge that for the sake of which noble youths go forth duly from a house to a houseless life, that is, the supreme end of the religious life, and having attained it will abide in it." Thereat the five monks said to the Lord, " By that exercise, friend Gotama, by that course, by that practice of austerity you did not attain the excellence of most noble knowledge and insight that surpasses human powers. Will you when you live in abundance, have given up exertion, and have turned to a life of abundance now attain the excellence of most noble knowledge that surpasses human powers ? " [Again he tells them that he is an arahat, and they put their question a second and a third time.]

Thereat the Lord said to the five monks, " Do you notice, monks, that I have never spoken to you thus before now ? " " Never thus, reverend sir." " The Tathāgata, monks, is an arahat, and has obtained complete enlightenment [etc. down to ' abide in it ']." So the Lord was able to convince the five monks. They listened again to the Lord, gave ear, and fixed their minds on the thought of insight.

THE FIRST SERMON

So the Lord addressed the five monks : These two extremes, monks, are not to be practised by one who has given up the world. What are the two ? The one, devoted to lusts and pleasures, base, sensual, vulgar, ignoble, and unprofitable, and the other devoted to self-mortification, painful, ignoble, and unprofitable. By avoiding these two extremes, monks, the Tathāgata has gained the enlightenment of the middle path, which produces insight, produces knowledge, and conduces to tranquillity, to higher knowledge, to enlightenment, to Nirvāṇa. And what, monks, is the middle path, of which the Tathāgata has gained enlightenment, which produces insight, produces knowledge, and conduces to tranquillity, to higher knowledge, to enlightenment, to Nirvāṇa ? It is the Noble Eightfold Way, namely, right view, right resolve, right speech, right action, right livelihood, right effort, right mindfulness, right concentration. This, monks, is the middle path, of which the Tathāgata has gained enlightenment, which produces insight, produces knowledge, and conduces to tranquillity, to higher knowledge, to enlightenment, to Nirvāṇa.

Again, monks, this is the noble truth of pain : birth is pain, old age is pain, sickness is pain, death is pain. Union with unpleasant things is pain, separation from pleasant things is pain, not obtaining what one wishes is pain, in short, the five groups of clinging to existence are pain. And this, monks, is the noble truth of the cause of pain : the craving, which leads to rebirth, accompanied by delight and passion, rejoicing at finding delight here and there, namely, the craving for lust, the craving for existence, the craving for non-existence. And this, monks, is the noble truth of the cessation of pain : that complete and trackless cessation of that craving, abandonment of it, relinquishment, release, and aversion. And this, monks, is the noble truth of the path that leads to the cessation of pain : this is the Noble Eightfold Way, namely, right view, right resolve, right speech, right action, right livelihood, right effort, right mindfulness, right concentration.

' This is the noble truth of pain.' Thus, monks, among doctrines unheard before, in me sight and knowledge arose, wisdom arose, knowledge arose, light arose.

' This noble truth of pain must be comprehended.' Thus, monks, amongst doctrines unheard before, in me sight and knowledge arose, wisdom arose, light arose.

' It has been comprehended.' Thus, monks, among doctrines unheard before, in me sight and knowledge arose, wisdom arose, knowledge arose, light arose.

' This is the noble truth of the cause of pain.' [The same

refrains are repeated with the statements that the cause must be abandoned and has been abandoned.]

' This is the noble truth of the cessation of pain.' [The same refrains are repeated with the statements that the cessation must be realized and has been realized.]

' This is the noble truth of the way that leads to the cessation of pain.' [The same refrains are repeated with the statements that the path must be practised and has been practised.]

And when, monks, in these four noble truths my due knowledge and insight with its three sections and twelve divisions was well purified, then, monks, I recognized that in the world with its gods, Māras, Brahmās, with ascetics, brahmins, gods, and men, I had attained the highest complete enlightenment. Knowledge and insight arose in me that my release of mind is unshakable. This is my last existence, now there is no rebirth.

Thus spoke the Lord, and the five monks with delighted minds expressed approval at the Lord's utterance.

(Vinaya, Mahāv., i. 6, 10.)

VII. THE ORDINATION OF YASA

THE following story is given in the Vinaya in explaining the rules for admission to the Order. The formula for admission to the state of layman is the Threefold Utterance :

> I go to the Buddha as a refuge,
> I go to the Doctrine as a refuge,
> I go to the Order as a refuge.

Yasa being free from attachment to the passions was ready to leave the world and receive the *pabbajjā*, "the going forth from the world". After this would follow the *upasampadā*, the ceremony of ordination, if the candidate had reached the age of twenty. This formal admission to the Order was afterwards entrusted to a committee of monks, and continues now as the regular form of admission.

Now at that time there was in Benares a noble youth named Yasa, son of a guild-master and delicately nurtured. He had three palaces, one for the cold season, one for the hot, and one for the season of rains. He spent four months in the palace of the rainy season attended by music-girls, and did not come down from the palace. So the noble youth Yasa attended, endowed and possessed of the five pleasures of sense once fell asleep sooner than usual, and afterwards his attendants fell asleep. All the night an oil-lamp was burning. Now Yasa the noble youth woke sooner than usual, and saw his attendants asleep, a lute in the arms of one, a tambour on the neck of another, a drum in the arms of another, one with dishevelled hair, another with drivelling mouth, some muttering. It was like a cemetery before his eyes. As he looked, his wretchedness broke out, and his mind became set with disgust. So the noble youth Yasa made this solemn utterance : "How oppressive, how afflicting."

Then he put on his gilt shoes, and went to the door of the house.
Superhuman beings opened the door, saying, " May no one put
an obstacle before Yasa the noble youth in his going forth from
a house to a houseless life." So he went to the city-gate.
Superhuman beings opened the gate, saying, "May no one put
an obstacle before Yasa in his going forth from a house to a
houseless life." So Yasa went to the Isipatana deer-park.

At that time the Lord had arisen at night as it was dawning,
and was walking in the open air. The Lord saw the noble
youth Yasa coming from afar, and on seeing him came down
from where he was walking, and sat down on the seat prepared
for him. Yasa the noble youth on drawing near to the Lord
made this solemn utterance : " How oppressive, how afflicting ! " So the Lord said to Yasa the noble youth, " Now this,
Yasa, is not oppressive, this is not afflicting. Come, Yasa, sit
down, I will teach you the doctrine." Then Yasa the noble
youth at the words, "This is not oppressive, this is not afflicting",
was elated and glad, and taking off his gilt shoes approached the
Lord, and having saluted him sat down at one side. As Yasa
the noble youth sat there, the Lord gave him a regular exposition
of this kind : he preached a discourse on alms, morality, heaven,
on the wretchedness, worthlessness, and impurity of lusts, and
the blessing of renunciation. When the Lord perceived that
the mind of Yasa the noble youth was prepared, softened, free
from obstacles, elated, and well disposed, then he preached the
most excellent teaching of the doctrine of the Buddhas : pain,
the cause, the cessation, the Way. And just as a clean cloth
free from stain duly takes the dye, even so in Yasa, as he sat
there, arose the pure unstained eye of the doctrine that whatever
is liable to origination is liable also to cessation.

Now the mother of Yasa the noble youth went up to the
palace, and not seeing him went to the guild-master, the house-

holder, and on approaching him said, "Your son Yasa, house-holder, is not to be seen." The guild-master sent out messengers on horseback in the four directions, and he himself went to the Isipatana deer-park. The guild-master saw the footprints of the gilt shoes, and seeing them he followed their traces. Now the Lord saw the guild-master coming from afar, and as he saw him coming he thought, "what if I were to effect such an exercise of psychic power that the guild-master sitting here should not see Yasa the noble youth sitting here". So the Lord effected such an exercise of psychic power. The guild-master approached the Lord and said, "perhaps the reverend Lord might see Yasa the noble youth". "Well, householder, sit down. Perhaps sitting here you might be able to see Yasa the noble youth sitting here." So the guild-master thinking, "surely sitting here I shall be able to see Yasa the noble youth sitting here", elated and glad saluted the Lord and sat at one side.

As he sat at one side the Lord gave him a regular exposition of this kind : he preached a discourse on alms, morality, heaven, on the wretchedness, worthlessness, and impurity of lusts, and the blessing of renunciation. Then the guild-master having seen, attained, mastered, and penetrated the doctrine, with his doubts and uncertainties dispelled, confident and dependent on no one else for the teaching of the Master, said to the Lord : "Wonderful, reverend one, wonderful, reverend one, just as if one were to set up what was overturned, or uncover what was hidden, or show the way to one who was lost, or put a lamp in the darkness—those with eyes see visible things—even so has the Lord preached the doctrine in many ways. I go, reverend one, to the Lord and to the doctrine and the Order of monks. May the Lord take me as a lay disciple from this day forth while life lasts, who have gone to him as a refuge." He was the first layman in the world received by the triple utterance.

Now Yasa the noble youth, while the doctrine was being taught to his father, contemplated the stage of knowledge thus perceived and thus understood, and his mind was entirely released from the corruptions (āsavas). So the Lord thought that as his mind was entirely released from the corruptions, it was impossible for him to return to a lower state and enjoy pleasures as he did before while he lived in a house. " What if I now make the exercise of my psychic power to cease?" Then, the Lord having done so, the guild-master saw Yasa sitting, and on seeing him he said, "Your mother, dear Yasa, is filled with lamentation and grief. Restore your mother to life." Yasa looked at the Lord, and the Lord said to the guild-master, "Now what do you think, guild-master, Yasa with imperfect knowledge and imperfect insight has seen the doctrine just as you have. He has contemplated the stage of knowledge thus perceived and thus understood, and his mind is entirely released from the corruptions. Do you think, householder, that Yasa can return to a lower state and enjoy pleasures as he did before while he lived in a house?" "No, reverend sir." "Yasa the noble youth, householder, with imperfect knowledge and imperfect insight has perceived the doctrine as you have, and on contemplating the stage of knowledge thus perceived and thus understood, his mind has become entirely released from the corruptions. It is impossible for Yasa the noble youth to return to a lower state and enjoy pleasures as he did before while he lived in a house." "It is gain, reverend sir, to Yasa the noble youth, it is great gain to Yasa the noble youth, that the mind of Yasa the noble youth should be entirely released from the corruptions. May the reverend Lord consent to take food to-day from me with Yasa the noble youth as a junior disciple." The Lord consented by his silence. So the guild-master, perceiving the consent of the Lord, rose from his seat, saluted the Lord, passing round him to the right, and departed. Then Yasa the noble youth, soon after the guild-master, the householder, was gone, said to the Lord, "Reverend sir, may I receive from the Lord the order of going forth (*pabbajjā*), may I receive admission to the Order (*upasampadā*)?" "Come, monk," said the Lord, "well taught is the doctrine, practise the religious life for the complete extinction of suffering." This was the ordination of that elder. At that time there were seven arahats in the world.

(*Vinaya, Mahāv.*, i. 7.)

VIII. THE NOVICE'S RULES AND THE LAYMAN'S FAST-DAY RULES

THE ten rules are said to have been given when two novices were admitted by Sāriputta. The first five are also binding on laymen, and for the monks the third rule means celibacy. On the fast-day the layman also keeps eight rules, i.e. the first nine of this list, the seventh and eighth being combined in one.

THE NOVICE'S RULES

I ENJOIN, monks, ten rules of training for novices, and these are to be learnt by the novices : (1) Refraining from taking life. (2) Refraining from taking what is not given. (3) Refraining from incontinence. (4) Refraining from falsehood. (5) Refraining from strong drink, intoxicants and liquor, which are occasions of carelessness. (6) Refraining from untimely food [i.e. after noon]. (7) Refraining from dancing, singing, music, and seeing shows. (8) Refraining from the use of garlands, scents, and unguents, which are objects of adornment. (9) Refraining from a high or large bed. (10) Refraining from accepting gold and silver.

(Vinaya, Mahāv., i. 56.)

THE LAYMAN'S FAST-DAY RULES

A noble lay disciple thus reflects : Throughout life the arahats shun and abandon taking life. Laying aside the use of a stick or a knife they live modest, full of kindliness, and compassionate for the welfare of all living creatures. I too to-day, for this night and day, shun and abandon taking life. Laying aside the use of a stick or a knife I live modest, full of kindliness, and compassionate for the welfare of all living creatures. With this part I imitate the arahats, and will keep the Fast-day. With this part the Fast-day is kept.

Throughout life arahats shun and abandon taking what is not given ; accepting and expecting what is given they dwell purely and without stealing. I too to-day, for this night and day, shun and abandon taking what is not given ; accepting and expecting what is given I dwell purely and without stealing . . .

Throughout life the arahats abandoning incontinence practise continence, living apart, and avoiding the village practice of sex-intercourse. I too to-day, for this night and day, abandon incontinence and practise continence, living apart, and avoiding the village practice of sex-intercourse . . .

Throughout life the arahats shun and abandon falsehood ; they speak truth ; they are truthful, trustworthy, and reliable, not deceiving people. I too to-day, for this night and day, shun and abandon falsehood, speaking truth, truthful, trustworthy, and reliable, not deceiving people . . .

Throughout life the arahats shun and abandon occasions of carelessness in strong drink, intoxicants, and liquor. I too to-day, for this night and day, shun and abandon occasions of carelessness in strong drink, intoxicants, and liquor . . .

Throughout life the arahats eat only at one mealtime,[1] abstaining from eating at night, and avoiding untimely food. I too to-day, for this night and day, eat only at one mealtime, abstaining from eating at night, and avoiding untimely food . . .

Throughout life the arahats refrain from occasions of dancing, singing, music, seeing shows, the use of garlands, scents, and unguents, which are objects of adornment. I too to-day, for

---

[1] This does not mean only once a day, but eating at the right mealtime, i.e. before noon.

this night and day, refrain from occasions of dancing, singing, music, seeing shows, the use of garlands, scents, and unguents, which are objects of adornment . . .

Throughout life the arahats shunning and abandoning a high or large bed use a low bed or couches or mats of hay. I too to-day, for this night and day, shunning and abandoning a high or large bed use a low bed or couches or mats of hay. With this part I imitate the arahats, and will keep the Fast-day. With this eighth part the Fast-day is kept.

(*Anguttara*, iv. 248.)

IX. THE EXHORTING OF SOṆA

THE following is an instance of the legendary matter which frequently occurs in the discourses.   Such portions evidently belong to a secondary portion of the tradition, but they do give a consistent picture of Buddha's method in dealing with individual characters.   A similar story is told of a novice who was bewildered by the multitude of rules, and decided to leave the Order.   The Master sent for him, and asked him if he thought he could keep three rules.   The man eagerly assented, and Buddha told him to guard the doors of body, speech, and mind, and to do no wrong in deed, word, or thought.

THUS have I heard : At one time the Lord dwelt at Rājagaha on the Vulture-peak hill, and at that time the elder Soṇa dwelt at Rājagaha in the Sīta wood.   Now the elder Soṇa was sunk in meditation, and the following reflexion arose in his mind : those who are the Lord's disciples live an energetic life.   I am one of them, but my mind is not entirely released from the corruptions (*āsavas*).   I find enjoyments in my family ; it is possible to enjoy enjoyments and yet do virtuous actions.   Now what if I abandon the training and return to a lower state, and while enjoying enjoyments do virtuous actions.   So the Lord knowing the reflexion that went on in the elder Soṇa's mind, as a strong man might bend his arm and stretch it out or stretch it out and bend it, straightway disappeared from the Vulture-peak hill and appeared face to face with the elder Soṇa in the Sīta wood.   The Lord sat on the appointed seat, and the elder Soṇa saluted the Lord and sat down at one side.

As he sat there the Lord said to him, " Is it not the fact, Soṇa, that when you were sunk in meditation this reflexion arose in your mind : those who are the Lord's disciples live an energetic life?   I am one of them, but my mind is not entirely released from the corruptions. I find enjoyments in my family ; it is possible to enjoy enjoyments and to do virtuous actions. Now what if I abandon training and return to a lower state, and while enjoying enjoyments do virtuous actions ?" "Even so, Lord." "What do you think, Soṇa, when you lived a household life, were you skilled in playing the lute ?" "Even so, Lord." "What do you think, Soṇa, when the strings of your lute were too tight, could it then give a sound or be played ?" "No, Lord." "What do you think, Soṇa, when the strings of your lute were too loose, could it then give a sound or be played ?" "No, Lord." "But, Soṇa, when the strings were neither too tight nor too loose but evenly tuned, could your lute then sound and be played ?" "Even so, Lord." "Even so, Soṇa, too great energy tends to over-excitement, and relaxing of energy tends to sloth. Therefore, Soṇa, do you apply yourself to evenness of energy and try to master evenness of faculties, and in this way attain your object." "Even so, Lord," the elder Soṇa replied to the Lord. Then the Lord having exhorted the elder Soṇa with this exhortation, like a strong man bending his arm and stretching it out or stretching it out and bending it, disappeared from the Sīta wood and appeared on the Vulture-peak hill.

Thus the elder Soṇa after a time applied evenness of energy and mastered evenness of his faculties, and so attained his object. Thus the elder Soṇa, abiding alone, secluded, vigilant, ardent, and resolute, in no long time, with that purpose for which noble youths duly go forth from a house to a houseless life, in this actual life himself realized by higher knowledge the supreme end of the religious life, and having attained it abode in it. He realized that rebirth is destroyed, the religious life has been led, done what was to be done, there is nothing more for this existence. And the elder Soṇa was one of the arahats.

Now the elder Soṇa after attaining arahatship thought that he would go to the Lord and in his presence declare his own attainment of knowledge.   So he went to the Lord, and having approached him and saluted him sat down at one side.   Thus seated the elder said to the Lord : " The monk, Lord, who is an arahat, who has destroyed the corruptions, who has lived the life, whose fetters of becoming are destroyed, and who is released with perfect knowledge, is intent on six objects : he is intent on self-abnegation, on seclusion, on freedom from malice, on the destruction of craving, on the destruction of grasping, and on freedom from bewilderment."

(*Anguttara*, iii. 374.)

X. THE WEAVER'S DAUGHTER

THE *Dhammapada* is a collection of 423 verses accompanied by a commentary, which gives an account of how each verse or group of verses came to be uttered. The following is the commentary on verse 174.

ONE day when the Master had arrived at Āḷavī, the inhabitants invited him, and gave alms. The Master giving thanks at the end of the meal said : " ' Uncertain is life, certain is death. Of necessity I must die, and my life ends in death. Life is unsure, death is sure.' Even so should one practise reflexion on death, for those who have not practised reflexion on death are in their last hour, like a man who is terrified at seeing a poisonous snake, and struck with fear they utter a cry of fear and perish. But they who have practised reflexion on death are like a steadfast man who has seen a poisonous snake from a distance, and taking it with a stick he throws it away, and is not terrified in his last hour. Therefore reflexion on death should be practised."

On hearing this exposition of the doctrine the rest of the people went away intent on their business. But a certain weaver's daughter, who was about sixteen years old, thought, " Ah ! wonderful is the teaching of the Buddhas. I ought to practise reflexion on death." And day and night she practised reflexion on death. The Master went from there and came to the Jetavana monastery, and the girl practised reflexion on death for three years.

Now on a certain day the Master, observing the world at dawn, saw the girl as she came within the net of his knowledge, and calling her to mind thought, " How may she be ? " And he had the knowledge that " This girl from the day that she heard my exposition of the doctrine has practised reflexion on death for three years. I will now go there and ask the girl four questions, and when she explains them I will express approval at each of the four points, and utter a verse. At the conclusion of the verse she will be established in the fruit of Entering the Stream, and on account of this the teaching will be profitable to the multitude."

With a retinue of five hundred monks he set out from the Jetavana, and by degrees came to the Aggāḷava monastery. The people of Āḷavī, hearing that the Master had come, went to the monastery and gave him an invitation. The girl also heard of the Master's coming, and thought, " surely my father and Lord and teacher, the full-moon-faced great Gotama Buddha, has come", and glad at heart she thought, " it is three years since I saw the golden-hued Master ; now I shall be able to see his golden-hued body, and hear his sweet, most excellent doctrine ". But her father going into her room said, " My daughter, some-one has ordered a robe from me, and a foot of it is not yet woven. I will finish it to-day. Get the shuttle ready for me quickly and bring it." She thought, " I want to hear the doctrine of the Master. My father calls me ; can I hear the Master's doctrine if I get the shuttle ready and bring it ? " Then she thought, " If I do not bring the shuttle my father might strike and beat me, so I will get the shuttle ready and give it to him, and afterwards I will hear the doctrine." So sitting down on a chair she prepared the shuttle.

The inhabitants of Āḷavī waited on the Master, took his bowl, and stood for him to give thanks. The Master thought, " The noble daughter, for whose sake I have come on a journey of thirty leagues, to-day does not take the occasion. When she takes the occasion I will give thanks," and he sat in silence. When the Master is silent, no one in the world of gods and men dares to say anything to him.

D

Meanwhile the girl prepared the shuttle, put it in a basket, took it to her father, and then went to the edge of the assembly looking at the Master. The Master raised his head and looked at her. At the sign of his looking she perceived, " the Master seated in such an assembly looks at me and expects my coming, even into his presence he expects my coming ". Setting down the shuttle-basket she went into the Master's presence. But why did the Master look at her? It would be thus that he thought, " If she goes and dies like the common people, her future state of existence will be uncertain, but if she comes into my presence and goes away after attaining the fruit of Entering the Stream, her future existence will be certain, and she will be born in the Tusita heaven." But there was no final liberation for her if she died on that day. She, understanding that she was being looked at, approached the Master, and entering within the six-coloured rays (of his halo) saluted him and stood on one side. And on her saluting the Master, who was seated silent in the midst of such an assembly, as she stood there, he said to her, " My girl, whence have you come?" "I do not know, reverend sir." "Where will you go?" "I do not know, reverend sir." "Do you not know?" "I know, reverend sir." "Do you know?" "I do not know, reverend sir."

Thus the Master asked her the four questions, and the multitude murmured, " See, for shame, this weaver's daughter talks with the All-enlightened One on whatever she wishes; surely, when she was asked whence she had come, she should have said, from the weaver's house, and when asked where she was going, she should have said, to the weaver's workshop." The Master silencing the multitude asked, " My girl, when you were asked whence you came, why did you say, 'I do not know'?" " Reverend sir, you know that I have come from the weaver's house, but in asking whence I have come you asked whence I have come in being reborn here, and I do not know whence I have come in being reborn here." So the Master said to her, "Well done, well done, girl, you have explained the question that I asked you," and expressing approval he asked further, "When you were asked where you will go, why did you say you did not know?" "Reverend sir, you know that I shall take the weaver's shuttle-basket and go to the weaver's workshop, but you asked me where I shall be reborn when I go hence, and I do not know where I shall be reborn when I go hence after death." Then the Master said to her, "You have explained also this question that I asked you," and a second time he expressed approval, and asked further, "And why did you say that you knew, when you were asked if you did not know?" "Reverend sir, I know that I shall die, and hence I spoke thus." So the Master said to her, "You have explained this question also," and expressing approval he asked further, "Why, when asked, 'do you know', did you say you did not know?" "I know that I shall die, reverend sir, but that I shall die at such and such a time, at night or day or at dawn, I do not know, and therefore I spoke thus." So the Master said to her, "You have explained this question also," and expressing approval a fourth time he addressed the assembly : "None of you knew what she said, and you only murmured. They who have not the eye of wisdom are blind, and they who have the eye of wisdom are seeing." So saying he spoke this verse :

> Blind and unseeing is the world,
> And few are those with insight here ;
> As a bird from a net released,
> But few are they who heaven attain.

When the teaching was ended, the girl was established in the fruit of Entering the Stream, and the teaching was also profitable to the multitude.

Then she took her shuttle-basket, and went back to her father. He had sat down and fallen asleep, and she without noticing handed him the shuttle-basket. The shuttle-basket knocked against the top of the beam of the loom, and fell, making a noise. He woke up, and seizing the loom dragged it along. The beam moved, struck her on the breast, and she fell down dead. Then her father looked at her fallen down with all her body blood-stained, and saw that she was dead. And great grief came upon him, and lamenting, " no one else can extinguish my sorrow ", went into the presence of the Master, and told him of the matter, saying, " Reverend sir, extinguish my sorrow." The Master consoled him, saying, " Sorrow not, for in the endless round of worldly existence, even as at the time of your daughter's death, the tears that have been shed are more than the four oceans," and he gave him a discourse on the end-lessness of worldly existence. The weaver with his sorrow decreased asked the Master for admission to the Order, and receiving admission in no long time he attained arahatship.

(Dhammapada, com. on 174.)

XI. BIRTH-STORY OF THE BLESSINGS
OF THE COMMANDMENTS

THE Birth-stories (*Jātaka*) consist of about 500 tales of the previous existences of Buddha. Each story is introduced by some incident occurring in the Master's life as Buddha, such as the backsliding of a monk or some act of merit among the faithful. Buddha then tells a story of the past, in which the actors in the previous life are usually the same as those whom he is exhorting, and in which Buddha himself as the Bodhisatta always occurs. The stories of the past are often folk-tales and beast-fables, much older in origin than Buddhism itself. They are not parables, but they hold the same place in the Buddhist moral teaching as do the parables of the New Testament. They were much used, like the *exempla* of the Middle Ages, in popular preaching, and are still thus used in Ceylon and other Buddhist countries.

In the following tale the idea of merit as consisting in the accumulation of good karma is one that the Buddhist ethics largely superseded. The principle, however, that keeping company with the good implies in some sense a sharing of goodness is a general ethical truth.

THIS story the Master told while living at the Jetavana about a faithful lay disciple. Now this faithful, believing, noble disciple, going one day to the Jetavana, came in the evening to the bank of the river Aciravatī. As the boatman had drawn up his boat on shore and had gone to listen to the doctrine, the disciple saw no boat at the ferry, and taking joy in meditating on the Buddha he went down to the river. His feet did not sink in the water. As though on dry ground he went, until he had gone half-way, when he saw waves. Then his joy in meditating on the Buddha became less, and his feet began to sink, but he again strengthened his joy in meditating on the Buddha, and passing over the surface of the water entered the

Jetavana, saluted the Master, and sat on one side. The Master exchanged friendly greetings with him, and asked, " Disciple, as you came along the road, did you come with little fatigue ? " He replied, " Reverend one, I took joy in meditation on the Buddha, and receiving support on the surface of the water, I have arrived as though walking on dry ground." The Master said, " Not you only, on remembering the virtues of the Buddha, received support, but long before, when a ship was wrecked in mid-ocean, laymen remembered the virtues of the Buddha, and received support." On being asked by the disciple, he told a story of the past.

Long ago, in the time of the perfectly enlightened Buddha, Kassapa,[1] a disciple who had entered the First Path, embarked on a ship with a householder who was a barber. The barber's wife said, " Sir, let his welfare and ill be your care," and put the barber in the hands of the layman. Now on the seventh day afterwards the ship was wrecked in mid-ocean. The two men alighted on one plank and reached an island. There the barber killed birds, cooked and ate them, and offered them to the layman. The layman said, " Enough for me," and would not eat. He thought, " In this place there is no other support for us than the three refuges," and fixed his mind on the virtues of the Three Jewels. Now as he was thus thinking, a nāga [2] king who had been born on that island changed his body into the form of a great ship. An ocean-god was the pilot. The ship was filled with the seven kinds of precious stones. There

---

[1] The Buddha immediately preceding Gotama. He is also called " of the ten powers " in order to distinguish him from other persons of the same clan name.

[2] Nāgas were superhuman beings represented in Indian sculptures as hooded snakes with several heads. They were capable of assuming any form.

were three masts of sapphire, the anchor was of gold, the ropes of silver, the planks golden. The ocean-god stood in the ship, and called, " Does anyone want to go to Jambudīpa [India] ? " The layman said, " We wish to go." " Then come and embark." He embarked and called the barber. The ocean-god said, " It is going for you, not for him." " Why ? " he asked. " He does not practise the virtues of the commandments, that is the reason. I have brought it for you, not for him." " Very well, I give him a share in my almsgiving, in my keeping the commandments, and in the meditation I have practised." The barber said, " Sir, I accept with joy." " Now I will take him," said the god, and putting him on board brought both men over the ocean and came to the river at Benares. By his supernatural power he produced wealth in the house of both of them, and said, " You should keep company with the wise, for if the barber had not kept company with this layman he would have perished in mid-ocean" ; and telling the virtue of keeping company with the wise, he spoke these verses :

> Behold, this is the fruit of faith,
> Of virtue and of sacrifice ;
> A nāga in a vessel's form
> Conveys the faithful layman home.

> Then with the good keep company,
> And with the good associate ;
> For through his friendship with the good
> The barber comes in safety home.

Thus the ocean-god standing in the air declared the doctrine and admonished them, and taking the nāga king went to his own abode.

The Master, after reciting this declaration of the doctrine, set forth the truths, and showed the connection of the birth.   At the conclusion of the truths the layman[1] was established in the fruit of those who return once to this world.   " At that time the layman[2] who had attained the First Path attained Nirvāṇa. Sāriputta was the nāga king, and I was the ocean-god."

(*Jātaka*, No. 190.)

---

[1] This was the layman who had crossed the river to see Buddha.

[2] The layman in the tale of the past.   The four stages are explained in the Introduction, p. 6.

XII. BIRTH-STORY OF THE KING OF RIGHTEOUSNESS

THIS birth-story is an illustration of the teaching which says, "Resist not him that is evil, but whosoever smiteth thee on the right cheek, turn to him the other also." But the virtue specially insisted on is heroism. This is one of six virtues which the Bodhisatta exercises in their perfection at different stages of his career, almsgiving, morality, patience, heroism, meditation, and wisdom. Hence they are known as the six Perfections. In later Pāli works these become a list of ten, with the addition of truth, resolution, love, equanimity.

LONG ago, when Brahmadatta was ruling in Benares, the Bodhisatta was born as the son of the chief queen. On his naming-day they gave him the name of prince Sīlava [i.e. the virtuous]. At the age of sixteen he had attained perfection in all branches of learning ; and afterwards on the death of his father he was established in the kingdom, and under the name of Mahāsīlava became a righteously ruling king. He built six almshalls, four at the four gates of the city, one in the middle, and one at his palace door, gave alms to poor travellers, kept the commandments, and performed the fast-day duties, being filled with patience, kindness, and compassion. As a parent cherishes a son seated on his hip, so he cherished all beings, and ruled his kingdom in righteousness.

Now one of his ministers misconducted himself in the harem, and this became commonly known. The ministers informed the king. The king inquiring into the matter found it out himself, and sending for the minister said, " Blind fool, you have acted wrongly, you are not worthy to dwell in my kingdom. Take your property, your wife and children, and go elsewhere." And he sent him forth from the country. The minister left the Kāsī country, and going to the king of Kosala gradually became a confidant of the king.

One day he said to the Kosala king, " Your majesty, the kingdom of Benares is like a honeycomb free from flies. The king is very mild, and with even a small military force it is possible to take the kingdom of Benares." The king on hearing his words thought, " The kingdom of Benares is great; can he be a hired robber in saying it is possible to take it with a small force ? " and he replied, " You are hired for this, I suppose." " I am not hired, your majesty, I speak the real truth; if you do not believe me, send me to waste a border village. When the men are taken and brought before the king, he will give them money and send them away." The king thought, " He speaks as a very brave man, I will test him then " ; and sending his men he caused them to waste a border village. The robbers were caught and brought before the king of Benares. The king on seeing them asked, " My children, why did you waste the village ? " " We cannot get a living," they said. " Then why did you not come to me ? Henceforth do not do the like again." And giving them money he sent them away. They went, and announced to the Kosala king what had happened. But notwithstanding this he did not dare to go, and again he sent men to waste the country in the middle of the kingdom. In the same way the king gave the robbers money, and sent them away. Notwithstanding this, however, he did not go, but again sent men to plunder in the very streets of Benares. The king gave money to these robbers also, and sent them away likewise. Then the Kosala king, seeing that he was a very righteous king, said, " I will capture the kingdom of Benares," and set out with an army.

Now at that time the king of Benares had a thousand invincible heroic warriors, who would not turn back from the advance of a mad elephant, intrepid even against the thunderbolt falling on their heads, and if king Sīlava wished it, able to subdue the whole of Jambudīpa. They, on hearing that the Kosala king was coming, approached the king, and said, " Your Majesty, the Kosala king is coming, saying he will take the kingdom of Benares ; let us go, and even before he has entered the border of our kingdom, smite him and capture him." " My children," he replied, " for my sake no suffering is to be inflicted upon others. Let those who want kingdoms take this." And he forbade them to go.

The Kosala king crossed the border, and entered the middle of the country. Again the ministers of the king of Benares approached him, and spoke as before, but the king again refused. The Kosala king stopped outside the city, and sent a message to king Sīlava, " Let him either resign his kingdom or give battle." The king on hearing sent the reply, " I have nothing to do with fighting ; let him take the kingdom." And again the ministers approached the king, saying, " Let us not allow the Kosala king to enter the city ; even outside the city let us smite and capture him." The king as before refused, and causing the city gates to be opened, sat with his thousand ministers round him on his throne in the great hall.

The Kosala king with a great army entered Benares. Not seeing even a single enemy he went to the door of the king's palace, and finding the doors open, ascended to the splendidly adorned royal hall, thronged with ministers, caused the guiltless king Sīlava who was seated there to be seized with his thousand ministers, and said, " Come, bind this king and his ministers with their hands tightly fastened behind their backs, and take them to a cemetery. Bury them in holes up to their necks, and so cover them with earth that they cannot move even a hand. At night the jackals will come and do to them what is fitting."

The men, hearing the command of the robber king, bound the king and his ministers with their hands tightly fastened behind their backs and took them away. Even at that moment king Sīlava harboured no thought of violence against the robber king, and there was not one of the ministers who, when being bound and led off, could disobey the king's word, so well disciplined was his assembly.

Then the king's men took king Sīlava and his ministers to a cemetery, and buried them in holes up to their necks, the king in the middle with the ministers on both sides. They placed them all in holes, scattered earth over, made it firm, and came away. King Sīlava addressed his ministers and exhorted them, " Give not way to anger against the robber king, but practise friendliness, my children."

Now at midnight the jackals came, thinking they would eat human flesh. The king and his ministers on seeing them gave a shout with one voice. The jackals fled in terror. Then they turned to look back, and seeing that no one was following came up again. A second time the men gave a shout. As many as three times the jackals fled away, and again looking back and seeing that not a single person was following, they thought, " These must be men sentenced to death " ; and they became bold, and when the shout was raised again they did not flee. The oldest jackal came up to the king, and the others approached the ministers. The king, who was clever in device, marked the jackal's approach, and as though giving him the opportunity to bite, threw back his neck, and as the jackal was biting seized his neck with his teeth, and held him firm as in a vice. Being held by the teeth of the king, who was strong as an elephant, the jackal firmly held by the neck, and being unable to free himself, was in fear of death, and gave a great howl. The other jackals, hearing his cry of pain, thought he must have been seized by some man, and not daring to approach the ministers they all fled in fear of their lives.

Through the king holding firmly to the jackal that he had seized the earth was loosened, as the jackal moved to and fro, and the terrified animal removed the earth with his four feet on the upper part of the king. Then the king seeing that the earth was loosened released the jackal, and moving to and fro with the strength of an elephant, got both hands free, and clutching the edge of the hole came out like a cloud driven before the wind, comforted the ministers, removed the earth, took them all out, and stood in the cemetery surrounded by his ministers.

At that time some persons had thrown away a corpse in the cemetery, and had thrown it on a boundary between the territories of two yakshas.[1] The yakshas, being unable to divide the corpse, said, "We cannot divide it, but king Sīlava is righteous, he will divide it and give it to us ; let us go to him." Taking the corpse and dragging it by the foot they went to the king and said, "Your Majesty, divide this and give it to us." "Well, yakshas," he replied, "I would divide and give it to you, but I am dirty ; I must first bathe." The yakshas through their magic power brought scented water prepared for the robber king's use, and gave it to king Sīlava for bathing. After he had bathed they brought and gave him clothes intended for the robber king. He put these on, and they brought him a box with the four kinds of scent with which he anointed himself, and then various kinds of flowers, placed upon jewelled fans in a golden casket. When he had adorned himself with the flowers, they asked, "Can we do anything else ?" The king

[1] A kind of goblin, *see* p. 80.

made a sign of hunger. They went and brought him food flavoured with various kinds of excellent essences, which had been prepared for the robber king, and king Sīlava, being bathed, anointed, dressed, and adorned, ate the food flavoured with the various kinds of excellent essences. The yakshas brought him scented drink in a golden cup and golden bowl, prepared for the robber king's use. Then he drank the water and rinsed his mouth, and as he washed his hands they brought him the robber king's betel, prepared with the five kinds of scent, and after he had chewed it they asked, " Can we do anything else ? "   " Go and bring the robber king's sword of state, which lies by his head-pillow," said the king ; and they went and brought this also. The king took the sword, set the corpse upright, and smote it from the middle of the skull downwards into two parts, and thus dividing it gave an equal part to each yaksha, and washing the sword he stood with it girded on.

Then the yakshas ate the flesh, and being well disposed and delighted in heart asked, " What else can we do for you, O king ? "   " Well then, by your magic power set me down in the robber king's royal bedchamber, and put these ministers again each in his own house." They replied, " Very well, your Majesty," and did so. At that time the robber king was lying asleep on his royal bed in the royal bedchamber. King Sīlava smote his stomach with the flat of his sword, as he lay asleep and unconscious. He awoke in a fright, and recognizing king Sīlava by the light of a lamp, arose from his bed, summoned his courage, and stood up and addressed the king, " O king, on a night like this, with the house guarded, the doors shut, and the place inaccessible owing to the guard set, how did you come with sword girded on and fully adorned to my bedside ? " The king recounted in full all the details of his coming. The robber king on hearing replied with agitated mind, " O king, I, although a man, did not know your virtue, but your virtues are known to fierce and cruel yakshas, devourers of flesh and blood ; no longer, O king, will I be an enemy to you, who are endowed with such virtue." Then on the sword he swore an oath, asked the king's pardon, caused him to lie down on the state bed, while he himself lay down on a small couch.

When it dawned and the sun rose, he caused a drum to be sounded, assembled all the trade-guilds, ministers, brahmins, and householders, and recounted before them the virtues of king Sīlava, as though he were making the full moon rise in the heavens. And again in the midst of the assembly he asked the king's pardon, delivered the kingdom back to him, and said, " Henceforth it shall be my charge to deal with robbers who rise against you. Do you rule your kingdom with me to keep guard." Then he passed sentence on the calumniator, and with his army departed to his own kingdom.

So king Sīlava, splendidly adorned, sat beneath the white umbrella on a golden throne, which had legs shaped like those of a deer, and as he beheld his glory he thought, " This great glory and the lives of these thousand ministers being saved would not have happened if I had not acted with heroism. It was by the power of heroism that I recovered this splendour that I had lost and saved the lives of my thousand ministers. Without abandoning one's desire one should show heroism, for thus the fruit ripens for one who practises heroism." And making a solemn utterance he spoke this verse :

> So should a mortal strive and strive,
> Let not the wise man be cast down ;
> This truth in my own fate I see,
> According as I wished it came.

Thus the Bodhisatta expressing his solemn utterance in this verse thought, "Ah! how in those that are endowed with virtue does the fruit of heroism ripen," and doing deeds of good throughout his life, passed away according to his deeds (karma).

(*Jātaka*, No. 51.)

XIII. BIRTH-STORY OF THE CITY WITH FOUR GATES

THIS birth-story was a very popular one, and was elaborated in several schools by Buddhist poets. It illustrates four of the five careers (*gatis*) in which an individual may be born: an inhabitant of hell, a ghost, an animal, a man, or a god. Ghosts in Hindu belief are those who have not received the due rites of burial, but by the Buddhists this state was developed into a special career in which certain crimes had to be expiated.

LONG ago in the time of Kassapa [1] of the ten powers there lived the son of a chief of guild-merchants who was worth eight hundred millions. His name was Mittavindaka. His parents had entered the first stage of the Noble Path, but he was vicious and unbelieving. After his father's death his mother, who managed the household, said to him, "My son, the state of man is hard for you to obtain; give alms, keep the command-ments, perform the fast-day vows, and hear the doctrine." He replied, "Mother, I have no wish to give alms and so on; tell me nothing of that. I shall go according to my karma." But, though he answered so, his mother, on a certain fast-day of the full moon, said to him, "My son, to-day is set apart as a great fast-day. Take upon yourself the vows to-day, go to the monastery, and hear the doctrine all night, and I will give you a thousand pieces of money." "Very well," he replied, and through desire for the money he took upon him-self the vows, ate an early meal, went to the monastery, and passed the day there; and at night, in order that not a word of the doctrine should reach his ear, he lay down in one place

[1] The Buddha who immediately preceded Gotama.

and fell asleep. Early next day he washed his mouth, and returning home sat down.

And his mother thought, "To-day my son after hearing the doctrine will come home early, bringing the elder who preached the doctrine," and she got ready gruel, and food hard and soft, prepared a seat, waited for his coming, and seeing him returning alone said, "My son, why have you not brought the preacher?" "I don't want a preacher," he said. "Then drink the gruel," she replied. "You promised me a thousand pieces," said he; "give them to me now. I will drink it later." "Drink it, my son; you shall have them afterwards." "I will drink it when I have got them." So his mother set before him the bundle of a thousand pieces. He drank the gruel, took the bundle, and trading with the money in no long time gained two millions.

Then he thought he would get a ship and trade. He did so, and said, "Mother, I am going to do trade with this ship." But his mother replied, "You are my only son; in this house there is plenty of wealth, and at sea there are many dangers. Do not go." He replied, "But I will go; you cannot stop me." She said, "My son, I will stop you," and took hold of his hand. But he pushed her hand away, struck her, caused her to fall down, shut her in, and went off by ship to sea.

The ship on the seventh day, because of Mittavindaka, became immovable in the deep. Lots were cast to find the unlucky person, and three times the lot was found in Mittavindaka's hand. So they gave him a raft, saying, "Let not many perish for the sake of this one," and they put him on the water. And at that very moment the ship sped on swiftly over the ocean.

Alighting on the raft he reached a certain island. There in a crystal palace he saw four female ghosts. For seven days they used to undergo pain, and then for seven days pleasure. For seven days he experienced with them divine bliss. Then, as they were going away for their punishment, they said, "Master, on the seventh day we shall come back. Until we come back do not be distressed, but stay here," and they departed.

But he being in the power of craving embarked on his raft, and again sailed over the sea, till he reached another island, and there found eight female ghosts in a silver palace. In the same way on another island he found sixteen in a palace of jewels, and in another thirty-two in a golden palace. And with them he experienced divine bliss. When the time came for these also to undergo punishment, he went again over the sea, and saw a city with four gates, surrounded by a wall. It was the Ussada hell, a place where many inhabitants of hell undergo the consequence of their deeds. But to Mittavindaka it appeared as a city beautifully adorned. He thought, "I will enter this city and become king." On entering he saw a being burning in hell, and supporting on his head a razor-wheel. But to him the razor-wheel on his head seemed like a lotus. The fivefold fetters on his breast seemed like a splendid breastplate, and the blood dripping from his body seemed like red sandal-wood ointment. The sound of lamentation seemed like the sound of sweet singing. Mittavindaka approached him and said, "Fellow, you have been wearing that lotus long enough, give it to me." "Friend, it is no lotus, it is a razor-wheel." "You say that because you don't want to give it to me." The inhabitant of hell thought, "My past karma must be exhausted, he must have come for having struck his mother, as I did." So he said, "Come, sir, take this lotus." And with these words he threw the razor-wheel on Mittavindaka's head, and it fell, crushing his skull. At that moment Mittavindaka recognized the razor-wheel, and he cried out, " Take your razor-wheel, take your razor-wheel." But the other disappeared.

Then the Bodhisatta [in his birth as king of the gods] with a great retinue passed through the Ussada hell, and arrived at that place. Mittavindaka on perceiving him said to him, " Master, king of the gods, this wheel has come down on my head, and is grinding it small like sesame seeds. What is the sin that I have done?" And he spoke two verses :

> Four gates this city do enclose,
> Of iron are the walls, firm-built ;
> Here am I hindered and confined ;
> What is the sin that I have done?

> See the doors are shut and bolted,
> And like a bird am I caged in ;
> What is the reason, Yaksha, tell me,
> Why am I smitten with this wheel?

The king of the gods to explain the reason spoke six verses :

> A hundred thousand didst thou get,
> And in addition twenty more ;
> When thy kinsfolk on thee had pity,
> Thou wouldst not to their words give ear.

> Thou wentest sailing o'er the sea,
> An ocean journey, hard to win ;
> So to the four thou didst arrive,
> And then the eight, and the sixteen.

> And from them to the thirty-two,
> Then to the wheel, too, greedy one,
> Thou camest, driven by greed, and now
> The wheel revolves upon thy head.

THE CITY WITH FOUR GATES

> The city, wide and hard to fill,
> Laden with greed thou didst approach ;
> Who for this city seek in lust,
> They shall be bearers of the wheel.

> They who do not forgo great wealth,
> They who will not search out the Way,
> Who will not set their minds upon it,
> They shall be bearers of the wheel.

> Ponder thy deeds, and thy great wealth consider ;
> Follow not greed, all vain and useless is it ;
> And heed the words of those who would thee pity.
> If thou art such, the wheel shall not approach thee.

Mittavindaka on hearing this thought, " This son of the gods knows exactly what I have done. He will also know how long I have to burn. I will ask him," and he spoke the ninth verse :

> How long upon my head, Yaksha,
> This torturing wheel will it abide ?
> Tell me how many thousand years ?
> I ask thee, Yaksha, tell to me.

Then the Great Being in reply uttered the tenth verse :

> Be thy torture short or lengthy,
> Mittavindaka, hear thou me :
> The wheel is thrown upon thy head,
> From here thou canst not free thy life.

Saying this the god went to his own place, and upon the other came great suffering.

(Jātaka, No. 439.)

XIV. THE UNDETERMINED QUESTIONS

THE undetermined questions are a list of problems which Buddha is said to have refused to answer. Hence it is sometimes said that Buddha rejected metaphysics. But the refusal applies only to this list of questions, and they do not embrace all metaphysical inquiries. Buddhism holds a position which involves various principles quite as metaphysical as these, and the question as to how far Buddhism involves metaphysics is largely a matter of words.

The problems (1) as to whether the universe is eternal and (2) whether it is infinite or not are cosmological problems still debated by the physicists. (3) The question about life and the body is one formulated by another school and not discussed at all by the Buddhists. (4) The question of the continued existence of a released person after death is put in such a way that there is no possible way of answering it. It is discussed more in detail in Ch. XVI.

THUS have I heard: At one time the Lord was dwelling at Sāvatthī, in the Jetavana monastery in the park of Anāthapiṇḍaka. Now the elder Māluṅkyāputta had retired in meditation, and this thought arose in his mind: these views have been left unexplained by the Lord, set aside and rejected: that the universe is eternal, that it is not eternal; that it is finite, that it is infinite; that life is the same as the body, that life is one thing and the body another; that a released person exists after death, that he does not exist after death, that he exists and does not exist after death, that he neither exists nor does not exist after death. These things the Lord does not explain to me; that he does not explain them does not please me, it does not suit me. I will go to the Lord and ask him about the matter. If the Lord will explain, I will practise the religious life with the Lord, but if the Lord will not explain, then I will

abandon the training and return to a lower state. [Mālunkyā-
putta goes and states his decision.]

"Now did I, Mālunkyāputta, speak thus to you, 'Come,
Mālunkyāputta, practise the religious life with me, and I will
explain whether the universe is infinite' [etc.]?" "No,
reverend sir . . ."

"Anyone, Mālunkyāputta, who should say, 'I will not lead
the religious life with the Lord as long as the Lord will not
explain to me whether the universe is eternal [etc.],' that person,
Mālunkyāputta, would die without its being explained by the
Tathāgata. Just as if a man had been wounded with an arrow
thickly smeared with poison, and his friends, companions, relatives, and kinsmen were to get an arrow-surgeon, and he were
to say, 'I will not have the arrow pulled out as long as I do
not know the man by whom I was wounded, whether he was
of the warrior caste, a brahmin, of the agricultural caste, or a
serf . . . what was his name and clan . . . whether he was
tall, short, or of middle height . . . whether he was black, or
dark, or the colour of a gold-fish . . . whether he came from
such and such a village or town or city . . . whether I was
wounded with an ordinary bow or a cross-bow . . . whether
the bow-string was of swallow-wort or bamboo-fibre or sinew
or hemp or of milk-sap tree . . . whether the shaft was from
a wild or cultivated plant . . . whether it was feathered from
a vulture's wing or a heron's or a hawk's or a peacock's or a
sithilahanu-bird's . . . whether it was wrapped round with the
sinew of an ox or a buffalo or a ruru-deer or a monkey . . .
whether the arrow was an ordinary arrow or a razor-arrow or
a barbed arrow, or an iron arrow or a calf-tooth arrow or one
of oleander leaf.' Without knowing all this, Mālunkyāputta,
the man would die.

"It is not on the view that the universe is eternal that the religious life depends, nor on the view that the universe is not eternal. Whether the view is held that the universe is eternal or that universe is not eternal, there is still rebirth, there is old age, there is death, there is grief, lamentation, pain, sorrow, and despair, the destruction of which even in this life I declare.

" It is not on the view that the universe is finite or infinite . . . that life is the body or that life is one thing and the body another . . . that a released person exists after death or does not exist after death . . . that he exists and does not exist after death or does not exist and does not not exist after death . . . There is still rebirth, there is old age, there is grief, lamentation, pain, sorrow, and despair, the destruction of which even in this life I declare.

" Therefore, Mālunkyāputta, consider as unexplained what I have not explained, and consider as explained what I have explained. And what, Mālunkyāputta, have I not explained ? Whether the universe is eternal [etc.]. And why have I not explained this ? Because, Mālunkyāputta, it is not useful, it is not concerned with the principles of the religious life, it does not conduce to aversion, absence of passion, cessation, tranquillity, higher knowledge, enlightenment, Nirvāṇa. Therefore I have not explained it.

" And what, Mālunkyāputta, have I explained ? ' This is pain,' have I explained, Mālunkyāputta. ' This is the cause of pain,' have I explained. ' This is the cessation of pain,' have I explained. ' This is the path that leads to the destruction of pain,' have I explained. And why, Mālunkyāputta, have I explained this ? Because this, Mālunkyāputta, is useful, it is concerned with the principles of the religious life, it conduces to aversion, absence of passion, cessation, tranquillity, higher knowledge, enlightenment, Nirvāṇa. Therefore, Mālunkyā-putta, consider as unexplained what I have not explained, and consider as explained what I have explained." Thus spoke the Lord, and with joy the elder Mālunkyāputta applauded the words of the Lord.

(Majjhima, i. 426 ff.)

XV. SERMON ON THE MARKS OF NON-SELF

THE following discourse is said to have been the second made to the five monks. It discusses the question of the self only from one point of view, the view then held in India that there is some one element in the self which remains without change and passes from birth to birth. This is the doctrine of the *ātman* as held by both Hindus and Jains. The discussion starts from the Buddhist analysis of the self into five elements : the body, sensation or feeling, perception, the other elements of will, etc., grouped as the aggregates (*saṃkhāras*), and consciousness. Each of these elements, consciousness as much as the rest, is liable to change to sickness and pain, and cannot be called the self. It is the whole changing combination which transmigrates, and continues to do so until their final dispersion with the attainment of Nirvāṇa.

THE body, monks, is without self. For if this body were the self, this body would not be subject to sickness, and it would be possible in the case of the body to say, 'let my body be thus, let my body be not thus'. Now because the body is without self, therefore the body is subject to sickness, and it is not possible in the case of the body to say, 'let my body be thus, let my body be not thus'.

Sensation is without self . . . Perception is without self . . . The aggregates are without self . . . [The same statement is made of each as in the case of body.]

Consciousness is without self. For if this consciousness were the self, this consciousness would not be subject to sickness, and it would be possible in the case of consciousness to say, 'let my consciousness be thus, let my consciousness be not thus'. And because consciousness is without self, therefore consciousness is subject to sickness, and it is not possible in the case of consciousness to say, ' let my consciousness be thus, let my consciousness be not thus '.

What do you think, monks, is the body permanent or impermanent ? " Impermanent, reverend one." But is the impermanent painful or pleasant ? " Painful, reverend one." But is it fitting to consider what is impermanent, painful, and subject to change as, ' This is mine, this am I, this is my self ' ? " No, reverend one." [And so of the other elements.] Therefore, monks, whatever body, past, present, or future, internal or external, gross or subtle, low or eminent, far or near, all this body is not mine, not this am I, not mine is the self. Even so is it to be looked upon in reality with right wisdom. [The same assertion is made of feeling, etc.]

Thus perceiving, monks, the learned noble disciple feels loathing for the body, for sensation, for perception, for the aggregates, for consciousness. Feeling loathing he becomes free from passion, through freedom from passion he is released, and in him who is released arises the knowledge, "I am released." He understands that rebirth is destroyed, the religious life has been led, done is what was to be done, there is nothing more for this existence. Thus, said the Lord, and the five monks with delighted minds expressed approval at the Lord's utterance. And when that exposition was being spoken the minds of the five monks were released without clinging from the corruptions. At that time there were six arahats in the world.

(*Vinaya, Mahāv.*, i. 6.)

XVI. THE SURVIVAL OF THE RELEASED

In the reply to Mālunkyāputta (Ch. XIV) the undetermined questions were put aside because they are useless to the disciple, and the views held by different schools are contradictory. But the question about the existence of a released person after death has a direct interest to the individual, and here in the reply to Vaccha it receives special treatment. It is shown that there is no possible way of giving a positive answer. Annihilation is certainly rejected, but existence as we know it is transient existence, becoming and passing away, and no statement can be made about one who has reached a state beyond anything that we know as existence. As the Lord said to Upasīva, "When all qualities are removed, all modes of speech are removed also."

THE view that the world is eternal, Vaccha, is a jungle of views, a wilderness, a theatrical show, a perversion, a fetter of views, and is coupled with suffering, destruction, despair, and pain, and does not tend to aversion, absence of passion, cessation, tranquillity, higher knowledge, enlightenment, Nirvāṇa.

The view that the world is not eternal, that the world is finite, not finite, that life is the same as the body, that a released person exists after death or does not exist or exists and does not exist or is neither existent nor non-existent, is a jungle of views . . . Considering it disadvantageous, Vaccha, I have accordingly adopted none of these views.

"But has Gotama any view?" "The Tathāgata, Vaccha, is free from views, for this is what the Tathāgata holds : body, the arising of body, the passing away of body ; feeling, the arising of feeling, the passing away of feeling ; perception . . . the mental aggregates . . . consciousness . . . Therefore the Tathāgata with the destruction, passing away, cessation, abandonment, and rejection of all imaginings, all agitations, all perverse conceit about a self or of anything belonging to a self, is released, thus I say."

"But, sir Gotama, where is the monk reborn whose mind is thus released?" "It does not fit the case, Vaccha, to say he is reborn." "Then, sir Gotama, he is not reborn." "It does not fit the case, Vaccha, to say he is not reborn." "Then, sir Gotama, he is both reborn and not reborn." "It does not fit the case, Vaccha, to say he is both reborn and not reborn." "Then, sir Gotama, he is neither reborn nor not reborn." "It does not fit the case, Vaccha, to say he is neither reborn nor not reborn." "In this matter, sir Gotama, I have got into a state of ignorance, a state of confusion, and the small amount of faith that I had in Gotama through a former conversation has now disappeared." "Enough of your ignorance, Vaccha, enough of your confusion, for deep is this doctrine, difficult to be seen and comprehended, good, excellent, beyond the sphere of reasoning, subtle, intelligible only to the wise. It is hard to be understood by you, who hold other views, another faith, other inclinations, another discipline, and have another teacher. Therefore, Vaccha, I will ask you this, and do you explain it as you may please. Do you think, Vaccha, that if a fire were burning before you, you would know that a fire was burning before you?" "If a fire were burning before me, sir Gotama, I should know that a fire was burning before me." "And if someone were to ask you on what the fire burning before you depends, how would you explain it?" "If asked, sir Gotama . . . I should explain it thus : this fire burning before me burns on account of the fuel of grass and sticks." "If the fire before you were to go out, would you know that the fire before you had gone out?" "If the fire before me were to go out, I should know that the fire before me had gone out." "And if someone, Vaccha, were to ask you, in what direction has the fire that was before you gone, to the east, west, north, or south, if you were thus asked, Vaccha, how would you explain it?" "It does not fit the case, sir Gotama, to say so, for the fire burned through depending on its fuel of grass and sticks, and through consuming this and not getting any other it is without food, and comes to be what is called extinct." "Even so, Vaccha, that body by which one might define a released person has ceased, it is uprooted, cut off like a palm-tree, made non-existent, and not liable to arise again in the future. A released person who is freed from what is called the body, Vaccha, is deep, immeasurable, hard to fathom, and like the great ocean. It does not fit the case to say he is born again, to say he is not born again, to say he is both born again and not born again or to say he is neither born again nor not born again." [The same statement is then made of each of the other elements of the individual, feeling, perception, the other mental aggregates, and consciousness.]

Thereat the wandering ascetic of the Vaccha clan said to the Lord, "Just as if, sir Gotama, there were a great sāl-tree near a village or town, and if through inconstant change its branches and leaves were to fall, the pieces of bark and fibrous wood; and later on with the disappearance of these branches, leaves, pieces of bark, and small fibre, it were to be established, pure in its strength; even so does this discourse of Gotama with the disappearance of branches and leaves, pieces of bark and small fibre, stand established, pure in its strength. Wonderful, sir Gotama, wonderful, sir Gotama, it is as if one were setting up what was overturned, or revealing what was hidden, or showing the way to someone who was lost, or putting a lamp in the dark—they that have eyes see visible things—even so has the doctrine been expounded by sir Gotama in many ways.

I go to sir Gotama as a refuge, and to the doctrine, and to the Order of monks. May Gotama take me as a lay disciple from this day forth, while life shall last, who have come to him for refuge."

(Majjhima, i. 485 ff.)

XVII. GOD AND THE SOUL

THE undetermined questions are here discussed from a different point of view in the *Brahmajāla-sutta*, "the Net of Brahmā", a discourse which is meant to include as in a net all possible ways of answering them. Among the problems there raised is the question whether the universe and the self (*ātman*) are eternal. The Hindu view is that the universe passes in cycles from rest to activity and back again to rest. Brahmā is held to be the creator in the sense that he sets the world going again. Buddhism accepted the theory of cycles, but with its doctrine that everything is impermanent denied that Brahmā is the cause of change. As the question of an absolute beginning was set aside there was no need to ask who set it going. But in this discourse we do find a denial of the belief that Brahmā was the prime mover. He is represented as a being in the Brahma world, who wishes to have companions, and then when other beings are born there he thinks he has created them.

The theory of an *ātman* is also attacked, the view that behind the self as perceived there is some permanent entity. It is this supposed entity that is attacked by the Buddhists, and replaced by the analysis of the self into five groups, as set forth in Chapter XV.

THERE are, monks, some ascetics and brahmins who are in part eternalists and in part non-eternalists, and who hold in four ways that the self and the world are in part eternal and in part not eternal. On what grounds do they hold this?

There is a time, monks, when at some period and occasion, at the end of a long age, this universe is evolving. As the universe evolves, beings mostly tend to be born in the Radiant world. There they exist formed of mind, feeding on joy, shining with their own light, moving through the air, dwelling in glory, and they abide for a long time.

There is a time, when at some period and occasion, at the end of a long age, the universe is running down. Then the abode of Brahmā appears empty. Now some being, owing to his life or his merit being exhausted, passes away from the Radiant world and is born in the empty Brahma world. There, formed of mind, feeding on joy, shining with his own light, moving through the air, dwelling in glory, he abides for a long time. Then from being alone for so long he feels uneasiness, discontent, and longing : " Would that other beings might come to this place." Then other beings owing to their life or merit being exhausted pass away from the Radiant world and are born in the Brahma world as companionship for that being. They too are formed of mind . . . and abide for a long time.

Then the being who was born there first thinks, " I am Brahmā, the great Brahmā, the supreme, the unsurpassed, the all-seeing, the controller, the Lord, the maker, the creator, the best disposer, the subjecter, the father of all that have been and shall be. By me these beings have been created. And why ? Because a while ago I thought, ' would that other beings might come here '. Such was my wish, and here these beings have come." And the beings themselves who have been born later think, " Surely this is Brahmā, the great Brahmā, the supreme, the unsurpassed, the all-seeing, the controller, the Lord, the maker, the creator, the best disposer, the subjecter, the father of all that have been and shall be. By the Lord Brahmā we have been created. And why ? We have seen that he was born here first, but we have been born after him."

Now, monks, the being who was born there first was longer lived and more beautiful and powerful, but the beings who were born later were shorter lived and less beautiful and powerful. A case occurs that one of these beings on passing away from that (Brahma) world comes to birth in the same world

again. Having done so he goes forth from a house to a houseless life. On going forth he applies exertion, he applies effort,
diligence, earnestness, and right reflexion, and realizes such concentration of mind that with concentrated mind he remembers
his immediately preceding birth, but nothing before that. He
says, " now this Brahmā, the great Brahmā, the supreme, the
unsurpassed, the all-seeing, the controller, the Lord, the maker,
the creator, the best disposer, the subjecter, the father of all
that have been and shall be, by whom we have been created,
he is permanent, stable, eternal, of unchangeable nature, and
will abide ever the same. But we who have been created by
that Brahmā are impermanent, unstable, short-lived, liable to
pass away after coming to birth here." This, monks, is the
first case on account of which and about which some ascetics
and brahmins who are in part eternalists and in part non-
eternalists hold that the self and the universe are in part eternal
and in part not eternal.

[Two other cases are given in which an individual in the
same way infers that some gods are eternal and others not.]

In the fourth case, with reference to what is it that some
ascetics and brahmins hold that the self and the universe are
in part eternal and in part not eternal ? In this case some
ascetic or brahmin is a reasoner, an investigator. Expressing
his theory, worked out by himself in accordance with reasoning and investigation, he says, " this self, which is called eye,
ear, nose, tongue, body, is impermanent, unstable, not eternal,
liable to change ; but the self called thought, mind, or consciousness is permanent, stable, eternal, not liable to change,
and it will abide ever the same ". This, monks, is the fourth
case on account of which and about which some ascetics and
brahmins hold that the self and the universe are in part eternal
and in part not eternal.

In this matter, monks, the Tathāgata knows that these particular theories, so held and taken up, will have such a result. This the Tathāgata knows, and he knows something better than that, and that knowledge does not affect him. As he is not affected, he sees peace [1] within, and having duly seen the rise and passing away of the sensations, the enjoyment and unpleasantness in them and escape from them the Tathāgata is completely released.

These are the things, monks, hard to see, hard to comprehend, tranquil, lofty, beyond the sphere of reasoning, abstruse, and to be apprehended only by the wise, which the Tathāgata having comprehended and realized himself makes known, and it is on account of these things that those who would speak rightly would properly praise the Tathāgata.

(*Dīgha*, i. 17.)

[1] *Nibbuti*, a synonym of Nirvāṇa. Rh. Davids says, ' way of escape '.

XVIII. DHANIYA THE HERDSMAN

BESIDES those portions of the Scriptures which are recorded as the direct words of the Master or of his disciples and those narrative portions, probably due to the reciters, which explain the time and place of their utterance, there are other still later groups. These are mainly collections of verses, and they have been included in the fifth Nikāya. They evidently belong to a period when there was a lively literary activity and an impulse to produce compositions according to accepted literary rules. The most important of these works is the *Sutta-nipāta* (Section of discourses). It includes poems with simple moral teaching, ballads recording various events in Buddha's life, and incidents in the life of the Order. Some are in dramatic or dialogue form as in the case of the following poem.

DHANIYA : I have boiled my rice, my milking have I ended,
On the banks of the river Mahī, with equals dwelling ;
Roofed is my house, my fire alight—
Then if it be thy wish, now rain, O sky.

THE LORD : I am free from anger, stubbornness have I ended,
On the banks of the river Mahī, for one night dwelling ;
Unroofed is my house, my fire is out—
Then if it be thy wish, now rain, O sky.

DHAN. : Here are no gadflies found to pester me,
In the meadows deep in grass the cattle wander ;
They can bear the rain when it shall come—
Then if it be thy wish, now rain, O sky.

THE LORD : Firmly bound is my raft and well-constructed,
To the farther side I have crossed, and left the torrent ;

Now no longer I need a raft—
Then if it be thy wish, now rain, O sky.

DHAN. : Dutiful is my wife, not wanton is she,
Long has she lived with me, the charming one ;
Naught that is bad do I hear of her—
Then if it be thy wish, now rain, O sky.

THE LORD : Dutiful is my mind, delivered is it,
Long has it been well-tamed and duly practised ;
Nought that is bad is found in me—
Then if it be thy wish, now rain, O sky.

DHAN. : Self-gained is my livelihood and my earnings,
My children, healthy, are gathered round about me ;
Nought that is bad do I hear of them—
Then if it be thy wish, now rain, O sky.

THE LORD : Of no one whatsoe'er am I the servant,
With what I earn through all the world I wander ;
No need to me is there of wages—
Then if it be thy wish, now rain, O sky.

DHAN. : I have cows, and I have calves,
Cows have I in calf, and cows for breeding ;
Also a bull have I, a lord of cattle—
Then if it be thy wish, now rain, O sky.

THE LORD : No cows have I, no calves have I,
No cows in calf have I, no cqws for breeding ;
Not even a bull is mine, a lord of cattle—
Then if it be thy wish, now rain, O sky.

DHAN. : The stakes are well rammed in, not to be shaken,
New are the ropes of munja-grass, well twisted ;
Nor will the calves be able to break through them—
Then if it be thy wish, now rain, O sky.

THE LORD : I as a bull have broken through the fetters,
Have crushed, as an elephant, the galucchi creeper ;
No more shall I a womb of existence enter—
Then if it be thy wish, now rain, O sky.

Then at that moment burst a mighty storm-cloud,
Filling the earth and deep expanse of ocean [1] ;
And hearing the raining of the sky,
These words did Dhaniya the herdsman utter :

" Gain in no wise small indeed is ours,
Who see the Lord endowed with eye of wisdom ;
To thee we come for refuge, seeing one,
Be thou to us the Master, O great Muni.

" Dutiful is my wife, and so am I,
May we in the Blessed One lead the holy life ;
And crossed to the further shore of birth and death,
So may we make an end of grief and pain."

MĀRA : He that is rich in sons delights in sons,
So he that is rich in cows therein delights ;
For in the passions is the delight of man,
He that is passionless finds no delight.

---

[1] Victor Henry takes it to be understood that the wealth of Dhaniya
is destroyed in the storm.

THE LORD : He that is rich in sons finds grief in sons,
So he that is rich in cows therein finds grief;
For in the passions is the grief of man;
He that is passionless is free from grief.[1]

(*Sutta-nipāta*, i. 2.)

[1] The last two verses occur elsewhere as a separate poem, and do not
properly belong here.

XIX. THE JEWEL DISCOURSE: A SPELL

As Buddhism did not deny the gods, but only their eternity, so it did not deny the existence of the many other supernatural beings that hold a place similar to the fairies and goblins of Western mythology, such as nāgas (Ch. XI), yakshas or yakkhas (flesh-eating goblins), gandharvas (heavenly musicians), and kinnaras (fairies). The belief in spells or incantations was equally strong. By appealing to the spirits in the name of the Triple Jewel—Buddha, the Doctrine, and the Order —their good influence and even conversion might be won, and by making offerings to them as alms one would certainly acquire merit.

ALL spirits whatever that are here assembled,
That haunt the earth or through the air are passing,
May all those spirits be well-disposed and kindly,
So may they hear this utterance with attention.

Therefore attend and hearken, all ye spirits,
Show kindness to the race of human beings,
Who bring to you by day and night their offerings ;
Therefore with vigilance grant them your protection.

Whatever wealth there may be here or yonder,
Or any perfect jewel in the heavens,
In no wise is it equal to the Buddha—
In the Buddha is this jewel of perfection,
So through this truth to us may there be welfare.

The state immortal, passionless, and perfect,
Won by the Sakya Sage in meditation,
Nought verily is there equal to that doctrine—

In the Doctrine is this jewel of perfection,
So through this truth to us may there be welfare.

The purity which the best of Buddhas lauded,
The meditation called uninterrupted,
Nought is there equal to that meditation—
In the Doctrine is this jewel of perfection,
So through this truth to us may there be welfare.

The persons eight,[1] commended by the righteous,
Who form four pairs, worthy are they of offerings,
The true disciples of the blessed Master,
Great is the fruit of gifts to them presented—
In the Order is this jewel of perfection,
So through this truth to us may there be welfare.

They who with firm mind have applied themselves,
Free from desire, to Gotama's instructions,
Their end attained, are plunged in the immortal,
Taking the free gift, and enjoy Nirvāṇa—
In the Order is this jewel of perfection,
So through this truth to us may there be welfare.

Like as a pillar at a city's threshold,
Firm in the ground, by the four winds unshaken,
So I affirm is the good man unshaken,
Who pondering on the noble truths perceives them—
In the Order is this jewel of perfection,
So through this truth to us may there be welfare.

[1] The persons in the four stages of the Eightfold Way (Introd., p. 6).
Each stage is divided into two degrees, the *way* and the *fruit*, forming
eight classes or four pairs.

They who to the noble truths apply themselves,
The truths well-taught by the profoundly wise one,
They, even though they be exceeding slothful,
Not to the eighth rebirth will be subjected—
In the Order is this jewel of perfection,
So through this truth to us may there be welfare.

Then when he verily attains to insight,[1]
Three things he wholly leaves behind and loses :
False theory of the self, uncertainty,
And all there is of ceremonial practice ;
From the four hells that person is delivered,
Nor can he then the six great crimes [2] commit—
In the Order is this jewel of perfection,
So through this truth to us may there be welfare.

Whatever act of wickedness the bhikkhu
In deed, or word, or thinking, has committed,
Impossible for him is its concealment,
Impossible for him who has seen the path—
In the Order is this jewel of perfection,
So through this truth to us may there be welfare.

As in a forest grove with tops in flower
In the first month, and in the first hot season,
So did he teach the best supremest doctrine,
The highest truth that leadeth to Nirvāṇa—

[1] Insight into the first truth, when he enters the stream and casts off the first three fetters.

[2] Murder of a mother, a father, an Arahat, shedding the blood of a Buddha, causing schism in the Order, following other teachers.

In the Buddha is this jewel of perfection,
So through this truth to us may there be welfare.

The Best One, he that knows, gives, brings the best,
The Highest taught the best supremest doctrine—
In the Buddha is this jewel of perfection,
So through this truth to us may there be welfare.

Destroyed is the old,[1] the new is not arisen :
They with their thought not set on future being,
The seeds destroyed, desire not germinated,
Like as this lamp the wise are thus extinguished—
In the Order is this jewel of perfection,
So through this truth to us may there be welfare.

All spirits whatever that are here assembled,
That haunt the earth or through the air are passing,
The Buddha let us reverence, the Tathāgata,
Worshipped of gods and men.   May there be welfare.

All spirits whatever that are here assembled,
That haunt the earth or through the air are passing,
The Doctrine let us reverence, the Tathāgata,
Worshipped of gods and men.   May there be welfare.

All spirits whatever that are here assembled,
That haunt the earth or through the air are passing,
The Order let us reverence, the Tathāgata,
Worshipped of gods and men.   May there be welfare.

(*Sutta-nipāta*, ii. 1.)

---

[1] Birth and rebirth.

XX. BUDDHA'S LAST MEAL

THE two following chapters are from the *Mahāparinibbāna-sutta*, the Great Discourse of the attaining of Nirvāṇa, which gives an account of the last few months of the life of Buddha and of his death. What the food was that Buddha ate at his last meal is disputed, but the oldest commentators definitely take it to have been soft boar's flesh. The word, however, is not the ordinary word for boar's flesh, and they mention other theories, one of which is that it was a kind of mushroom. There is no reason why it should not have been flesh, as meat-eating was permissible under three conditions, that the recipient had not seen, heard, or suspected that it was intended for him.

The actual nature of Buddha's illness has been discussed by Dr. Henry F. Stoll, M.D., of Hartford, Conn., and he holds that it was a case of coronary thrombosis such as may follow a heavy meal.[1]

THE Lord after staying at Bhoganagara as long as he wished, said to the elder Ānanda, "come, Ānanda, we will go to Pāvā". "Even so, reverend one," the elder Ānanda replied to the Lord. Then the Lord with a great retinue of monks proceeded to Pāvā. There the Lord dwelt at Pāvā in the mango-grove of Chunda the smith. Now Chunda the smith heard that the Lord had arrived at Pāvā, and was dwelling in his mango-grove. So Chunda approached the Lord, and having saluted him sat down on one side. As he sat on one side the Lord instructed, aroused, incited, and gladdened him with a discourse on the doctrine. Then Chunda the smith, instructed, aroused, incited, and gladdened by the discourse on the doc-

[1] *The American Heart Journal*, vol. 9, p. 412, 1934.

trine, said to the Lord, "Let the reverend Lord accept food from me to-morrow with the retinue of monks." By his silence the Lord assented. So Chunda the smith, perceiving the assent of the Lord, arose from his seat, saluted the Lord, and passing round him to the right went away.

So Chunda the smith the next day caused to be prepared in his house excellent food hard and soft, and much soft boar's flesh, and caused it to be announced to the Lord, "It is time, reverend sir, the meal is ready." So the Lord in the morning dressed himself, took his bowl and robe, and with the retinue of monks went to the abode of Chunda the smith. On arriving he sat on the appointed seat, and said to Chunda the smith, "Serve me, Chunda, with the soft boar's flesh that has been prepared, and serve the retinue of monks with the other hard and soft food prepared." "Even so, reverend sir," replied Chunda the smith, and served the Lord with the boar's flesh prepared, and the retinue of monks with the other hard and soft food. Then the Lord addressed Chunda the smith, "The boar's flesh that remains bury in a pit. I see no one in the world of gods and men, with Māra, Brahmā, with ascetics and brahmins, gods and men, by whom it could be eaten and properly digested, except by the Tathāgata." "Even so, reverend sir," replied Chunda, and, burying the remaining boar's flesh in a pit, he approached the Lord and having approached he saluted the Lord and sat down on one side. As he sat on one side, the Lord instructed, aroused, incited, and gladdened him with a discourse on the doctrine, and then arose from his seat and departed.

Then there arose in the Lord, after he had eaten the food of Chunda the smith, sharp pain and flow of blood, and violent mortal pains set in. Conscious and self-possessed the Lord endured them without anxiety, and said to the elder Ānanda,

" Come, Ānanda, let us go to Kusinārā." " Even so, reverend sir," the elder Ānanda replied to the Lord.[1]

(*Mahāparinibbāna-s.*, iv.)

[1] While resting on the way he told Ānanda that Chunda was to be told not to feel remorse for having given the Tathāgata his last meal. It was alms equal in merit to the meal that he received before his enlightenment, and conduced to long life, beauty, happiness, fame, heaven, and lordship.

XXI. THE DEATH OF BUDDHA

KUSINĀRĀ, to which Buddha journeyed after recovering from his sickness, has been identified with Kasia some 80 miles east of Kapilavatthu. The stages of trance (*jhāna* or *dhyāna*) are here part of the legend, but they are also real states of mind attained by the monk in his practice of meditation. (See Ch. V.) *Jhāna* is not mere musing but concentration of mind, in which outer sensations are shut off with the attainment of more and more intense stages of inner experience. It is this practice which, in China as *Ch'an* and in Japan as *Zen*, has developed into a sect that disregards dogmatic teaching, and places its whole discipline on mystic meditation.

Now the Lord with a great assembly of monks crossed to the farther bank of the river Hiraññavatī and came to Kusinārā, to the sāl-grove in the exercise-ground of the Mallas. Having come he thus addressed Ānanda : " Come, Ānanda, prepare for me between the twin sāl-trees a bed with its head to the north. I am sick, Ānanda, I will lie down." " Even so, Lord," the elder Ānanda replied to the Lord, and prepared a bed with its head to the north between the twin sāl-trees. Then the Lord lay down on his right side, arranging one foot on the other, mindful and conscious.

[Here follows a conversation with Ānanda on the four places of pilgrimage, and on the four kinds of persons worthy of a funeral mound. He consoles Ānanda, and when Ānanda wishes him to attain Nirvāṇa in a great city, explains the former greatness of Kusinārā. A wandering ascetic, Subhadda comes, and Buddha converts him as the last disciple. He gives instruction on certain points of discipline, and then addresses the monks for the last time.]

Then the Lord addressed the monks : "It may be, monks, that even a single monk may be in doubt or uncertainty about the Buddha or the Doctrine or the Way or the course of conduct. Ask, monks. Do not with regret say afterwards, 'The Master was face to face with us, and we could not ask the Lord face to face.'" At these words the monks were silent. [A second time and a third time the Lord thus addressed them.] And even a third time the monks were silent. Then the Lord addressed the monks : "It may be, monks, that out of reverence for the Master you do not ask. Let a friend tell it to his friend." At these words the monks were silent. Then the elder Ānanda said to the Lord, "Wonderful, reverend one, marvellous, reverend one. Thus is it my faith, reverend one, that in this assembly of monks there is not a single monk who is in doubt or uncertainty about the Buddha or the Doctrine or the Way or the course of conduct." "With faith you speak, Ānanda, but it is with knowledge, Ānanda, that the Tathāgata knows that in this assembly there is not a single monk who is in doubt or uncertainty about the Buddha or the Doctrine or the Order or the Way or the course of conduct. For in this assembly of five hundred monks the lowest monk has entered the stream, is not liable to be born in a lower state of existence, is sure, and destined to enlightenment." Then the Lord addressed the monks : "Well now, monks, I address you. Impermanent are compound things ; strive with earnestness." These were the last words of the Tathāgata.

Then the Lord reached the first trance. Rising from the first he reached the second trance. Rising from the second he reached the third trance. Rising from the third he reached the fourth trance. Rising from the fourth trance he reached the stage of the infinity of space. Rising from the attainment of the infinity of space he reached the stage of the infinity of consciousness. Rising from the attainment of the infinity of consciousness he reached the stage of nothingness. Rising from the attainment of the stage of nothingness he reached the stage of neither perception nor non-perception. Rising from the attainment of the stage of neither perception nor non-perception he reached the stage of the cessation of perception and feeling.

Then the elder Ānanda said to the elder Anuruddha, " The Lord has attained Nirvāṇa, reverend Anuruddha." " The Lord has not attained Nirvāṇa, Ānanda, he has attained the stage of the cessation of perception and feeling."

Then the Lord passing from the attainment of the cessation of perception and feeling attained the stage of neither perception nor non-perception. Passing from the attainment of neither perception nor non-perception he reached the stage of nothingness. Passing from the attainment of the stage of nothingness he reached the stage of the infinity of consciousness. Passing from the attainment of the stage of the infinity of consciousness he reached the stage of the infinity of space. Passing from the attainment of the stage of the infinity of space he reached the fourth trance. Passing from the fourth trance he reached the third. Passing from the third trance he reached the second. Passing from the second trance he reached the first. Passing from the first trance he reached the second. Passing from the second trance he reached the third. Passing from the third trance he reached the fourth. Passing from the fourth trance the Lord straightway attained Nirvāṇa.

When the Lord attained Nirvāṇa, with the attaining of Nirvāṇa, there was a great earthquake, terrifying and frightful, and the drums of the gods resounded. When the Lord attained Nirvāṇa, with the attaining of Nirvāṇa, Brahmā Sahampati uttered this verse :

> All beings in the universe
> Shall lay aside their compound state;
> Even so a teacher such as he,
> The man unrivalled in the world,
> Tathāgata with the powers endowed,
> The Enlightened has attained Nirvāṇa.

When the Lord attained Nirvāṇa, with the attaining of Nirvāṇa, Sakka, king of the gods, uttered this verse:

> Impermanent alas! are compounds,
> They rise up and they pass away;
> Having arisen then they cease,
> And their quieting is bliss.

When the Lord attained Nirvāṇa, with the attaining of Nirvāṇa, the elder Anuruddha spoke these verses:

> No breathing in or out was there
> Of him with firm-established heart,
> Free from all motion, winning peace,
> When he the great sage passed away.

> Then he with heart released from clinging
> Controlled and bore his suffering;
> As the extinction of a flame,
> Even so was his mind's release.

When the Lord attained Nirvāṇa, with the attaining of Nirvāṇa, the elder Ānanda spoke this verse:

> Then was a terrifying awe,
> Then was a horrifying dread,
> When he of all the marks possessed,
> The Enlightened had Nirvāṇa reached.

When the Lord attained Nirvāṇa, some of the monks there

who were not free from passion threw up their arms and lamented, and fell suddenly to the ground and rolled about. " Too soon has the Lord attained Nirvāṇa, too soon has the Blessed One attained Nirvāṇa, too soon has the Eye in the world passed away." But the monks who were free from passion, mindful and thoughtful, endured it (with the thought) " Impermanent are compound things, what else is to be had from this ? "

Then the elder Anuruddha addressed the monks : " Enough, friends, grieve not, lament not. Was it not said long ago by the Lord that from all dear and pleasant things there is manifoldness and deprivation and change ? What else is to be had from this ? Verily there is no possibility that of anything born and produced and compounded and liable to destruction one could say, ' Do not go to destruction.' "

(Mahāparinibbāna-s., v.)

INDEX

93